We all need help in stretching our incomes or family budgets to keep up with today's astronomical cost-of-living increases. George and Marjean Fooshee know, from their own experience and that of people George has counseled, that there is a way to "beat the money squeeze." Discover the honest facts about your family's finances. Find out how to realistically evaluate your expenditures, isolate your areas of overspending and cut back on unnecessary expenses. Learn from YOU CAN BEAT THE MONEY SQUEEZE how you and your family can target the source of your money problems and be totally free from financial worries.

You Can Beat the Money Squeeze

George and Marjean Fooshee

Power Books

Fleming H. Revell Company
Old Tappan, New Jersey

Scripture verses identified KJV are from the King James Version of the Bible.

Scripture quotations identified NIV are from HOLY BIBLE New International Version, copyright ©, New York International Bible Society, 1978. Used by permission.

Scripture quotations identified LB are from The Living Bible, Copyright © 1971 by Tyndale House Publishers, Wheaton, Illinois 60187. All rights reserved.

Scripture quotations identified NEB are from The New English Bible. © The Delegates of the Oxford University Press and the Syndics of the Cambridge University Press 1961 and 1970. Reprinted by permission.

Scripture quotations identified RSV are from the Revised Standard Version of the Bible, copyrighted 1946, 1952, © 1971 and 1973.

Scripture quotations identified NAS are from the New American Standard Bible, Copyright © THE LOCKMAN FOUNDATION 1960, 1962, 1963, 1968, 1971, 1972, 1973, 1975 and are used by permission.

Poem in chapter two from Jack R. Taylor, *God's Miraculous Plan of Economy* (Nashville: Broadman Press 1975) p. 95. Used by permission.

Quotation from HOW TO SUCCEED WITH YOUR MONEY by George M. Bowman. Copyright 1960, 1974. Moody Press, Moody Bible Institute of Chicago. Used by permission.

Chapter nine, previously titled "S'mores: Christian Stewardship," was first printed as an article in the *Evangelical Friend*. Permission to reprint granted.

Table 4 is reprinted from the January 5, 1979 issue of *The Holt Investment Advisory,* by special permission; © 1979, T. J. Holt & Company, 290 Post Road West, Westport, Ct. 06880.

Table entitled "Our Financial Goals" is from *You Can Be Financially Free* by George Fooshee, Jr. Copyright © 1976 by George Fooshee, Jr. Published by Fleming H. Revell Co. Used by permission.

Ziggy cartoons ZIGGY Copyright 1977 Universal Press Syndicate. Text Copyright 1977 American Greetings Corp. Reprinted by permission.

Library of Congress Cataloging in Publication Data

Fooshee, George.
  You can beat the money squeeze.

  Bibliography: p.
  1. Finance, Personal.   I.   Fooshee, Marjean, joint author.   II.   Title.
HG179.F572   332'.024   79-26309
ISBN 0-8007-5030-6

Contents

TO Wink and Lynn Nolte,
who have lived and taught
God's financial principles
better than anyone we know

Preface: That You Might Have Hope

The phones keep ringing! The letters keep coming! "May I come to see you?" "I've got troubles!" Voices desperate, tight, worried. People with money problems: tense, fearful, pressured, SQUEEZED.

But isn't the economy great? Hasn't our country just come through one of the greatest and longest expansion periods in history? Haven't we bought 54,000,000 cars and trucks and built 6,862,000 new houses in the past four years? Hasn't our GNP gone from 1.4 trillion dollars to 2.2 trillion dollars? That's an increase of 36%! Hasn't the median family income gone from $12,836 in 1974 to an estimated $19,000 in 1979? That's an increase of 48% in just five years.

We're *rich,* yet we're poor! The economy is great if you leave out the *me.* And families are squirming, with two wage earners bringing home insufficient money to pay the bills and hack at the debts.

How could we have avoided such a mess? How did we get this way? How can we get back to where we were before we "prospered" so much? How can we get unsqueezed?

Explore these four scriptural principles. You'll see how the Bible can keep you from being squeezed and how to get UNSQUEEZED.

- Get the facts
- Stay out of debt
- Keep records
- Spend sensibly

This book will deal with those four principles in a number of ways. We'll discuss debts, cars, housing, and other topics. To help you practically, we'll answer many questions people have asked about finances. And we have an added special feature which looks like this:

Marjean's 2¢: To Help You Get Unsqueezed

My wife, Marjean, will offer some sage advice, from her own experiences, on the various topics through this format. She has shared my vision for Christians to be financially free, has encouraged me in my ministry, and has worked with me in the finances of our marriage. These little asides have an important contribution to make to this book.

In our financial seminars, we often ask people what goals they have for the day. The ones most frequently listed are these:

- To set up a household budget and stick to it
- To be able to recognize the signs of getting into financial trouble, before the trouble gets too bad
- To learn how to be good stewards and use sound principles to manage all that God has given us
- To learn how to pass these principles on to our children, so that they could begin now to manage well
- To learn how to save more money
- To know how to get out of debt
- To be financially free and better use what income God has allowed us to earn
- To learn how to manage money so that it is not wasted

Almost everyone who comes to us for financial counseling wants to reach some or all of these goals. You're probably reading this book in order to reach such goals. This book was written to help you avoid the financial SQUEEZE and to become and stay financially free, to the glory of God.

Acknowledgments

To a loving mother, Lola Fooshee, for her faithful prayers for us.

To John and Jan LaFever, whose relationship with us is so special.

To Bettye Jane Fite, who encouraged and typed, encouraged and edited, and encouraged and corrected every word.

To Lynn Nolte and Ann Dobson, participants, with Marjean, in preparing special financial teaching for women, who enjoy sharing the Christian life together and delight in being helpers to their husbands.

To John Johnson, of the American Collectors Association, whose vision has enlarged ours.

To Max and Sandra Barnett, Brett and Mary Yohn, Bob and Sandie Anderson, Baptist Student Union directors at Oklahoma, Nebraska, and Kansas State Universities, who have lived these principles and taught them to hundreds of young people.

To Lloyde Johnson of Better Book Room, Inc., for his outstanding service to us and our community.

To Bill Shell, who edited and organized our manuscript.

To Gene Warr, for his helpful counsel.

To those who asked the questions, who came for counsel, and who turned from the world's money way to follow God's principles.

We express our love and appreciation.

Introduction: The Squeeze We All Face

People cry on our couch. They shuffle their feet in my office. They talk nervously over the phone. Their usual net-worth statement looks something like this:

Assets

Cash	$ 50
Savings	
Stocks & bonds	
House	42,000
Furnishings	4,000
Cars	3,800

Liabilities

	Total Debt	Monthly Payments
Mortgage	$38,000	$380
Finance company (cars)	3,200	150
Credit cards	1,800	90
Medical bills	600	50

Their income looks great with both of them working: a gross of over $18,000 annually.

After Social Security taxes of $1,103 on the $18,000, and Federal and State taxes of $2,361, the take-home pay has shrunk to $14,536. After a tithe of $1,800 and payments on the mortgage and other debts of $8,040, this amount has decreased to $4,696. That $4,696 is what's left for food, clothes, cars, health needs, gifts, life insurance, household expenses, utilities, vacations, savings, and educational expenses. Can you imagine meeting these expenses out of $391 a month? You'd cry, too! One lady was crying when she called my office and said, "Mr. Fooshee, is there any hope for me?"

The Hard Facts

What's happened? Haven't our incomes been increasing at rapid rates? Isn't your family making more now than you ever thought you'd be earning?

Here's what's happening:

	Median Family Income
1970	$ 9,867
1978	$17,400
Increase	$ 7,533

So our incomes have increased 76%. Great!

Not so great! The average price of a new house:

1970	$23,386
1978	$67,600
Increase	$44,214
Percent increase	189%

And that's two and one-half times faster than the median family income. Is it any wonder that over one-half of American families who could qualify to buy the average-priced new house in 1970 can't qualify to buy one today?

Then there are taxes:

1970   Social Security on median income = 4.8% of first $7,800 of the $9,867 = $374.40

1978   Social Security on median income = 6.05% of the whole $17,400 = $1,052.70.

Dollar Increase = $678.30

That's a 181% increase.

Federal Taxes

1970   on median family income of $9,867 = $1,094

1978   on median family income of $17,400 = $1,910

That's a 75% increase.

Let's look at what's left of the median family income after taxes.

	Income	Social Security & Federal Tax	Spendable
1970	$ 9,867	$374 + $1,094 = $1,468	$ 8,399
1978	$17,400	$1,053 + $1,910 = $2,963	$14,437
	$ 7,533		$ 6,038
	(Income up 76%)		(Spendable up 72%)

I call it a SQUEEZE!

The Apostle Paul may have expressed how many feel today: ". . . We were under great pressure, far beyond our ability to endure, so that we despaired even of life. Indeed, in our hearts we felt the sentence of death. But this happened that we might not rely on ourselves but on God, who raises the dead" (2 Corinthians 1:8, 9 NIV).

The Bible is a book of hope. And the good news is that you can avoid the SQUEEZE or become UNSQUEEZED by applying four biblical principles to your life: "For everything that was written in the past was written to teach us, so that through endurance and encouragement of the Scriptures we might have hope" (Romans 15:4 NIV). The four biblical principles to avoid the SQUEEZE or to become UNSQUEEZED are:

1. Get the facts
   a. on debt
   b. on cars
   c. on houses
   d. on spending

2. Stay out of debt
   a. Trust God or trust a loan?
   b. What about home mortgages?
   c. Credit cards: Are they sinful?
   d. College loans?
3. Keep records
   a. Benefits
   b. Burdens
   c. Blessings
   d. How to do it
4. Be a sensible spender
   a. Super savers
   b. Several shortcuts
   c. Sizable salvages
   d. Stashing

Get the Facts

A widow in my church came to me for counsel. She had just received an offer for some property she owned, and since the amount seemed attractive and the realtor was in a hurry to complete the deal, she was inclined to accept it. Before closing the sale, however, she had seen another realtor, who had offered her $500 more than she had first been offered. Because the first offer had come from a good friend of her deceased husband, she was confused. That's when she called me.

I counseled her: Get the facts. Hire a reputable appraiser (I gave her the name of one) and pay him what he asks for the appraisal. Find out—on the basis of other sales in the area, current property values in the community, and several other factors—about what the property should be worth.

She did. Her property was worth $3,000 more than the highest offer! She offered the property to the man who made the first offer and promptly sold it for 10% more than his original offer.

My friend did not decide before getting the facts. She followed Solomon's advice to her profit: "What a shame—yes, how stupid!—to decide before knowing the facts!" (Proverbs 18:13 LB).

The Scriptures present the get-the-facts principle often. In the incident of the feeding of the five thousand, we read this exchange between Jesus and the disciples:

> But he answered, "You give them something to eat."
> They said to him, "That would take eight months of a man's wages! Are we to go and spend that much on bread and give it to them to eat?"
> "How many loaves do you have?" he asked. "Go and see."
> When they found out, they said, "Five—and two fish."
>
> Mark 6:37, 38 NIV

In answer to the generalities of the disciples, Jesus was saying specifically, "What do we have? Get the facts, men!"

An Old Testament illustration of the principle is found in the account of the widow whose husband had died and who was paying his debts (2 Kings 4). The price was either immediate payment or the repossession of her two sons as slaves. (Boy, how bill collecting has changed!) The distraught woman came to Elisha with a clear question, "What shall I do?" Elisha's reply was a clear get-the-facts question, ". . . How much food do you have in the house?" (2 Kings 4:2 LB). In both situations God multiplied what they had to meet the need—feeding the crowd and paying the debt.

Most of the financial counsel I offer involves starting where people are, with what they have, and doing what they can. Sounds simple. But it isn't. Every person who calls me for counsel gets the same treatment. He is sent a simple Net-Worth Statement. "Just give me the facts of your situation," I tell him. "When you send the facts in, I'll call and make an appointment with you."

I never hear from over 75% of the people who initially call, seeking my help. They aren't willing to get the facts in their own situation. If they aren't willing to take that first step and send back a net-worth statement, then I'm not willing to meet with them.

A sign on an IBM executive's office says: IF YOU DON'T GET THE FACTS, THE FACTS WILL GET YOU. My observation is that the facts are getting many in financial trouble. Four areas of personal finance stand out as the trouble spots: debt, cars, houses, and budgets. You'll be as amazed as I've been to see the results of getting the facts in each area.

Marjean's 2¢: Get the Facts

My friend Ann was out shopping one day. She was looking through several items of clothing. When the saleslady asked, "May I help you?" Ann replied, "No thanks, I am just getting the facts." She was following the get-the-facts principle by doing some comparison shopping.

I try to do this each week, by reading the newspaper on the day the grocery ads come out. I compare the ads of three stores before planning my menus for the week. When making my grocery list according to my needs, I can take advantage of the best buys.

By knowing the facts before going to the store, I save time and money in my shopping. I have also discovered the least crowded times to shop. I avoid Friday afternoon, Saturday, and late afternoon of any weekday. From 1:00 P.M. to 2:00 P.M. Monday through Thursday seem to be the best times in the stores where I shop.

Get the facts in your community.

---

1 *Dealing With Debt's Deadly Squeeze*

Have you ever seen smoking listed as one of the leading reasons for divorce? Have you read that someone committed suicide and left a note saying that smoking was the cause of his despondency? Probably not! But you may be familiar with the label that's always included with cigarette ads: WARNING! THE USE OF THIS PRODUCT MAY BE INJURIOUS TO YOUR HEALTH.

You may be using an item that contains no such warning label from the Treasurer of the United States. Look at your credit cards. Do you see anywhere on them any warnings such as these?

> Warning! The use of this product may cause tension in your marriage. It may make you irritable. It could lead to severe depression. It could cost you a job opportunity. It may enslave you forever. It may, in the future, cause a drastic change in your life-style.

On many credit cards, however, this true but seldom-noticed statement is printed on the back: "Customer by retaining or using this card agrees to be bound. . . ." Being caught in the debt trap is in great contrast to the purpose God has for our lives. "For I am the Lord your God who brought you out of the land of Egypt, with the intention that you be slaves no longer; I have broken your chains and will make you walk with dignity" (Leviticus 26:13 LB). The result of credit-card spending is usually the binding up of one's finances with a continual round of interest and payments that never seem to stop.

The Debt Trap

The Bible expresses real caution about traps: "When a bird sees a trap being set, it stays away, but not these men; they trap themselves! They lay a booby trap for their own lives" (Proverbs 1:17, 18 LB).

The characteristics of a trap are that it is:

- attractive
- easy to get into
- almost impossible to escape from

No wonder debt is called a trap. The characteristics of debt fit its definition so well.

But God does not want His people in bondage: ". . . and you will know the truth, and the truth will set you free" (John 8:32 LB).

Our local newspaper once summed up the debt trap in a dramatic headline: "Easy Credit Way to Financial Hell."

Let's look at the easy part of credit. All that is required is to say, "Charge it," or to hand over a plastic card. What could be simpler? No money changes hands. You don't even have to think much about the cost of what you've spent.

My experience with families is that, if they are not keeping records, they are overspending. One man reported to me that when he finally decided to tally up his debts, he was astounded to find out he owed over $10,000 as a result of constant overspending.

The following tables will show you the result of credit-card mania. Would you have any trouble spending $80 more than you make each month? Table 1 shows what adding $80 a month, or $960 per year, to your debt will total in just five years, at a compound-interest rate of 18%.

Table 1: Debt Addition

Year	Debt Addition	Interest	Total Debt
1	$960	$173	$1,133
2	960	377	2,470
3	960	617	4,047
4	960	901	5,908
5	960	1,236	8,104

Remember the warning that isn't on your credit card? The one the well-known store does not issue on their revolving charge account: "The use of this card may cause a drastic change in your life-style"!

To repay an $8,000 debt, in approximately the same length of time it took to accumulate it, at $960 per year, takes an annual payment of $2,438 per year. You can be out of debt in five years at the $2,438-per-year repayment.

Table 2: Debt Repayment

Year	Payment	Interest	Balance Due
1	$2,438	$1,350	$6,912
2	2,438	1,142	5,616
3	2,438	894	4,072
4	2,438	582	2,216
5	2,438	222	—

What has the debt accumulation of $960 per year for five years cost?

Interest first five years	$3,304
Interest last five years	$4,190
Total interest	$7,494

The $960 debt accumulated each year, for five years, cost you an average annual interest of $749 for the ten-year period. And that's the cost in money.

But note the cost in trauma. Here's the situation. To go $80 per month into debt, the family simply refused to live within its income. Now, to escape the trap, they must take the following two dramatic, life-style-changing actions: They must stop overspending $80 a month. Having said *yes* to spending and debt, they must now learn to say *no* to debt, go on a cash-only plan, and do without the $80 each month they used in credit. *Plus:* The repayment of borrowing plus interest will require another dramatic change in life-style—an additional $203.15 per month. To pay off the $8,000 accumulated in five years of overspending, the $203.15 payment will need to be made for the next five years. Adding the two reductions in spendable income ($80 + $203.15) produces a $283.15 change in their standard of living. In my experience not many folks are able to do it. But God is a God of hope and One who helps us do it.

The Debt Set

Texaco has a "Travel Card."

TWA calls theirs a "Get Away Card."

Master Charge prints on theirs: "The Interbank Card."

My own bank puts out "The 24-Hour Money Card."

Changing Times magazine recorded this statement: "A fellow wrote in with a painless system for making ends meet. It's ready to go as soon as you can Master Charge your Bank Americard bills." The same magazine raised this question: "Is it true today's soldiers are taught if captured to give only their name, rank, Master Charge number and expiration date?"

Banks are making debt so easy that a whole new type of checking account has been created. A billboard on a Dallas freeway proclaimed in large print the name of their miracle account:

THE GOOF-PROOF

OVERDRAFT

ACCOUNT

Other names for this account in my area are: reserve account, balance plus checking, and money management. These accounts enable you to plunge into debt simply by writing checks for more money than you have in your account. Suddenly you've been loaned money (usually in $50 increments) to cover the overdraft. And you didn't have to fill out papers with all sorts of embarrassing questions about your income, debts, and other personal finances.

Christmas in America has become a season in which special movies are released with much ballyhoo. The 1978 biggie was *Superman*. Wichita's Master Charge, not to be outdone, announced: "It's *Supergift!*" Partial descriptive phrases in the ads were: "A gift that forever solves the 'What to Give' problem. . . . The perfect gift for everyone. . . . A gift better than cash. . . . You pay for it at your convenience." The summary phrase meant to persuade you to use this miracle gift is, "So next time you're stuck three weeks from payday, trying to decide how and what to give, don't settle for an average gift. Make it a *Supergift!*" What was a *Supergift?* A gift certificate from Master Charge that allowed the recipient to buy from any place that accepts Master Charge. When it was used, the giver's account was charged for the gift, as a cash advance, with an immediate interest charge to the giver's account.

When I see such ads, my heart grieves. So many people

Marjean's 2¢: *Marjean's Super Gift*

How thrilled I was when I received a box of hand-painted note cards with my initials, flowers, and cute little animal caricatures. These notes were lovingly drawn on a pad of plain paper, by a close friend of mine. I very carefully selected them to send to special people who would appreciate the individually decorated notes.

The same idea could be adapted by buying an inexpensive pad of paper and package of envelopes. Decorate them with pictures carefully cut out of old greeting cards or magazines and pasted on the front of the folded note paper. Or, if you happen to be artistic (try your hand), decorate the notes with some marking pens.

Anyone would be thrilled to receive such a personalized gift. Any number of ideas for practical and inexpensive gifts are available. Try your creativity, have fun, and save money. That's my idea of a Super Gift!

---

believe that credit cards, charge accounts, and overdraft accounts can solve their gift problems, make Christmas a joy, and forever solve their money woes. *But God* has such a clear, specific formula for paycheck management. The

Bible says, ". . . make do with your pay!" (Luke 3:14 NEB). The violation of this checkbook formula transforms the Debt Set into the Debtor Set.

"Forgive Us Our Debts"

Our Lord's Prayer contains the well-known, often-prayed phrase ". . . forgive us our debts . . ." (Matthew 6:12 KJV). Our government and the vast majority of Americans act as though the simple utterance of that phrase erases the penalty of past borrowing and allows them to go right on overspending. The astronomical growth of the federal debt in recent years will show how, collectively, we are failing to be content with our wages.

Table 3: Federal Debt in Billions

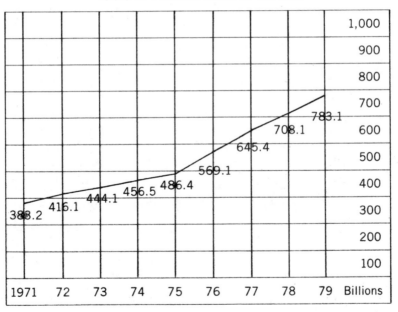

Inflation is rated by most Americans as our number-one problem. Many economists feel that the federal government's borrowing to meet its budget is a primary cause of inflation. Voters are expressing their disfavor with runaway government budgets, leading to larger and larger deficits. The biblical principle of owing no man anything (Romans 13:8) should apply to governments as well as to individuals.

Nineteen seventy-eight was to be a year when the long economic expansion would run its course. According to the prognosticators, the American economy was heading into a recession. Early in 1979, newspapers all over the country had headlines similar to my own local paper:

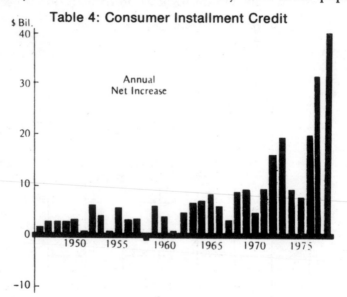

Table 4: Consumer Installment Credit

Consumer installment debt outstanding continued to rise at an alarming rate during 1978. This helped gloss over some of the economy's more glaring imbalances. Debt increases have to decelerate in 1979, however, helping initiate a severe economic contraction.

"Economy Strong, Employment Up, No Recession Yet." What happened? What fueled the expansion beyond 1978? *Borrowing!* Joe Consumer used his credit cards, revolving charge accounts, and finance-company loans at a record-breaking pace, leading to a phenomenal increase in his debt.

Table 4 reveals the additions to consumer debt in recent years. Note that 1978 additions were twice those of 1976. Individually we have been violating the make-do-with-your-pay principle in the same reckless way as our government spenders.

Why are people willing to mortgage more and more of their future earnings? Because we've been gripped with a new spending philosophy. Such a philosophy seems to be the only way to fight the battle against inflation. I call it the inflation mentality (*see* chapter two).

Questions
ON DEBT

1. Is there a time in your early life when you will be more in debt? My experience is that debt becomes a habit. The choice is between debt and no debt. Once the line is crossed from no debt to debt, people seldom pay off their charge accounts. The minute the car is paid off, the question is, "What can we buy with those payments we've been making?"

A friend of mine was given a bottle of champagne for his wedding. With it came a card that read, "Don't open this until you are out of debt." My friend laughingly told me that, after fifteen years of marriage, the champagne was still unopened.

2. How can a person in a low-income bracket ($10,000), with two or three children, provide the necessities of living without going into debt? The question includes part of the answer. With or without debt, persons of very low incomes will probably provide only the *necessities* of living and not the *niceties* of living. To borrow to provide such necessities only means less money in the future, when payments and interest come due.

3. *Would a debt-free population cause an economic depression in the country?* Most certainly! If our government quit overspending its income by the average $54 billion it has gone into debt during each of the last three years, the economy would certainly suffer. And if consumers began to pay off the $256 billion in consumer debt, while not adding the 1978 increase of $40 billion, the economic ripples would be felt throughout the world. But don't hold your breath! It's almost like saying, "If every Christian tithed . . . ."

4. *What do you think about the national debt?* I think that, corporately, we're violating biblical principles. Someday we'll reap what we've sown for our greed. "So each of us shall give account of himself to God" (Romans 14:12 RSV).

5. *Do you recommend debt-consolidation loans to pay off your bills, if you also change your spending habits?* I do not recommend borrowing as a way of getting out of debt. You just can't borrow your way out of debt. Transferring debt from high interest to lower interest may make sense. If a person owed on several accounts charging 18% interest, I've seen cases in which borrowing from his credit union at 12% to pay off the 18% accounts made sense. Most credit unions maintain insurance which pays off the credit-union loan in case the borrower dies or becomes disabled.

6. *Aren't you overlooking two factors in counseling people to keep out of debt? By being in debt, but paying regularly, I keep a good credit rating, in case of emergencies. In addition, the interest I pay really costs a lot less, since it is deductible from my income tax.* I prefer to be prepared for emergencies with savings rather than credit. Does the

Bible glorify the ant (Proverbs 30:24, 25) because it has good credit? No! The ant stores up food for the winter. The ant is a saver.

As for those tax deductions, I prefer to list giving deductions rather than interest deductions. If Marjean and I had paid interest on our cars and major purchases for these twenty-five years of marriage, our giving to the Lord's work would have been thousands of dollars less.

ON CREDIT CARDS

1. Is it wrong to use credit cards? I hope not, since I carry many of them when I travel. There's a big difference between using a credit card for *credit* and using it for *debt*. The user for credit is not overspending, and he knows it. Funds are available to pay each bill when the statement arrives. No finance charges are ever paid.

The user for debt is overspending, and he knows it. When the statement arrives, he'll be fortunate to have the money to pay the minimum amount due. So he'll pay the maximum interest.

One man in a California seminar told the audience that he "hadn't used his credit cards since Christmas."

"Has that been a help?" I asked.

"Golly, yes," he replied. "Otherwise I'd owe at least one thousand dollars."

2. What do you think of credit cards for most people? Since Americans owed $50 billion to credit-card companies in October 1979, I think that the cards were too great a temptation for most people to handle.

ON CREDIT

1. How do you establish credit without violating financial principles? The real question is: How do I develop a good credit rating and/or obtain a credit card?

Here are several steps you can take which may result in the establishment of a good credit record at your credit bureau:

a. Establish a satisfactory checking account at your local bank. Attempt to maintain a minimum balance of at least $100 at all times. Do the same for a savings account. When your banking relationship has been established, you may apply for a bank credit card through your bank. If you don't receive the card, the bank will tell you the reason. Then you will know future steps to take.

b. When you have saved the money for an item you wish to purchase, you're ready for another step. Let's assume that you want to buy a home appliance costing between $50 and $200. Place the money that you have saved in a savings account at your bank. Go to one of the national chain stores that advertise credit. Try to buy the item on an installment contract where you pay one-third or one-half as a down payment and the balance in three or four monthly installments.

When each payment is due, withdraw the money from your savings account. The interest you pay the store will undoubtedly be more than what you earn on your savings, but this difference will be your cost for establishing credit.

c. Another way is to visit a locally owned clothing, shoe, or department store where your family may be known. Request a charge account with a small $50 to $100 limit and use it for a small credit purchase. Pay the account off in two or three payments from your savings.

d. After completing your payments, ask the credit bureau to establish a credit file on you. Do this by person or by mail. The information requested from you will include at least the following: your full name, spouse's name, present and former addresses, present and former employment, date of birth, and Social Security number. List the credit account you just paid off, along with the account number.

e. You may request from the local credit bureau a copy of your file so that you know that a record has been established in your name. You'll probably pay a small fee for the record, but you'll be certain that you now can have your credit checked.

2. How can we buy a house, if we've never established credit? People have told me for years that if they don't have a good credit record, they can't buy a house. A credit-bureau manager once told me that no credit is the same as bad credit.

Several savings-and-loan executives dispute those statements. They've told me that they are interested in the prospective buyers' bank accounts, income, and certainly their debt obligations. A family with no debt (and possibly no credit record) and with money saved, is impressive. Such a family has made plans for the future. Their absence of debt means that they can handle larger house payments than the family which is loaded with debt payments.

Don't borrow money just to establish a credit record to buy a house. It's not necessary.

On Cosigning

1. What is wrong with a father's cosigning a note for his son to buy a car, as a teaching device for the son? Three things are wrong:

a. Cosigning violates Scripture: Proverbs 6:1–5; 11:15; 17:18; 20:16; 22:26; 27:13.

   b. You are teaching your son to borrow for things and violate the keep-out-of-debt principle.

   c. If you end up having to pay for the car, it's likely to cause bitterness and strained relationships (Hebrews 12:15).

2. What percentage of cosigners lose? A recent financial publication stated that 80% of all cosigners have to pay back those notes they cosigned. Bitterness is often the result.

3. What about cosigning with a son or daughter for college education? Our collection-agency personnel have contacted hundreds of cosigners about paying the college debts of their children. Their reactions are almost universally those of resentment, bitterness, and hostility toward us for even thinking that they should honor their signature and pay back the loan.

4. If cosigning violates Scripture, is lending money also against biblical principles? The Bible commands us to be lenders (Deuteronomy 15:11; Psalms 37:26; 112:5; Matthew 5:42; Luke 6:35). However, we are not to take advantage of our Christian brothers by charging interest for loans (Exodus 22:25; Leviticus 25:36; Deuteronomy 23:19).

ON INTEREST AND LENDING MONEY

1. Can you shed some light and share what the Lord has taught you concerning putting money away at interest, in light of Scriptures on usury? Is it scriptural to put money in a savings account, certificate of deposit, or other interest-bearing transactions, knowing that the bank loans it out to others, at interest? The Bible tells God's people to be savers. There is no question but that we aren't to spend it all, but to save some. The question is whether, biblically, we can entrust our funds to the moneylenders who will pay us interest on our money. Income from loaning money is usually called *usury* in the Scriptures. Today *usury* refers to unlawful or unjust rates.

The Bible cautions against charging interest to "the poor" and "your brother" and says that we shouldn't crush our debtors with high interest rates (Psalms 15:5).

The Scriptures do not oppose lending at interest. The warnings are with reference to our willingness to lend to the needy, expecting nothing in return (*see* Luke 6:34). And we are not to take advantage of a poor person with the possibility of gain for ourselves (*see* Proverbs 28:8).

The Bible allows interest to be charged for people's wants rather than their needs. Since most credit users are making no effort to be financially free, charging them interest for their desire to have things now is not in violation of Scripture.

2. Jesus said, "Give to him who begs from you, and do not refuse him who would borrow from you" (Matthew 5:42 RSV). Is this contrary to sound financial principles? The best answer to this question I've seen is William Barclay's comment, in *The Gospel of Matthew,* on this verse:

> Are we then to say that Jesus urged upon men what can only be called indiscriminate giving? The answer cannot be given without qualification. It is clear that the effect of the giving on the receiver must be taken into account. Giving must never be such as to encourage him in laziness and in shiftlessness, for such giving can only hurt. But at the same time it must be remembered that many people who say that they will only give through official channels, and who refuse to help personal cases, are frequently merely producing an excuse for not giving at all, and are at all times removing the personal element from giving altogether. And it must also be re-

membered that it is better to help a score of fraudulent beggars than to risk turning away the one man in real need.

3. *Is it Christian to sell on credit?*   This question must be resolved, through prayer, for the Lord's leading for every laborer. Is it Christian to sell—period? Food? Many people abuse themselves by overeating the food they buy. TV sets? Need I comment? For every item sold, there is the possibility of helpfulness or harm. Personally, I can collect bills people didn't pay, but I'd not want to sell new cars on credit. Nor could I work in a finance company and lend money for high interest rates.

4. *What are your views on lending money to friends?*   It is a quick way to lose friends and get rid of enemies. This sounds funny, but experience proves that it is true. More seriously, I've found out that lending individuals money when they've gotten themselves in a financial bind is an almost certain way to interfere with or postpone the work God is doing in their lives.

2 *Squeezing Through Inflation*

The most difficult questions asked today concern inflation. Most of these boil down to two:

- How does one plan for or handle inflation?
- Saving sounds great, but with inflation a known fact, don't we lose money by saving it, instead of being in debt and paying back with cheaper money?

As Christians, we face choices in our money management: Will we handle our money the world's way, or the biblical way?

Some quotes from a recent book that suggest ways to fight inflation are:

Avoid paying your bills for as long as possible.
Don't be ashamed to flirt on the ragged edge of being a dead beat.

The world's way is to borrow all you can on things that will cost more later. As inflation accelerates, you pay back the loans with cheaper dollars.

Early in 1979 an American businessman in England filed the largest personal bankruptcy ever recorded: $209 million. He had followed the borrow-on-property strategy to beat inflation and get rich. He got into trouble when he was unable to pay off his debts, because unexpected things happened that affected his income.

Life-Styles for These Times

God's way, on the other hand, involves these principles:

1. *Recognize God as the owner of all we have.* The whole world is His! We are only stewards, managers, and caretakers of it: ". . . for all the world is mine, and everything in it . . . . I want you to trust me in your times of trouble, so I can rescue you, and you can give me glory" (Psalms 50:12, 15 LB).

2. *Live as a giver.* Whatever we have, God wants us to return a portion to Him, in recognition that we acknowledge His ownership and trust Him.

The best guarantee against inflation that I've found in the Bible is in Malachi 3, an often-quoted chapter on giving. After we're told to be givers, the prophet gives us this promise from God:

> "Your crops will be large, for I will guard them from insects and plagues. Your grapes won't shrivel away before they ripen," says the Lord of Hosts. "And all nations will call you blessed, for you will be a land sparkling with happiness. These are the promises of the Lord of Hosts."
>
> Malachi 3:11,12 LB

Inflation eats away at the value of our money just as insects and plagues eat away at crops. Handling money God's way enables Him to guard the resources I manage for Him.

3. *Live as a saver.* The ant is singled out in Scripture for special mention because of storing up food for the winter (Proverbs 30:24, 25). The ant is a saver. Solomon said that the wise man is a saver, but the fool spends all his money (Proverbs 21:20). The Bible tells us to be savers and that God will bless our obedience in this area.

4. *Keep out of debt.* (*See* Romans 13:8.) In God's economy, the furniture is on the ceiling. Biblical principles are the opposite of the devil's schemes. Live on what you make. Trust God to meet your needs, instead of trusting loans. You'll find the Lord far more trustworthy to meet present and future needs than any loan you could trust for that purpose.

5. *Keep a budget.* (*See* 1 Corinthians 14:40.) A spending plan will help you keep control of your financial situation. You'll be prepared for the unusual. You'll plan to give, save, and spend. You'll be able to know how to adjust to the unexpected in both income and spending needs.

6. *Work.* The Apostle Paul sums up the biblical principle of work as follows: ". . . work heartily, as serving the Lord and not men" (Colossians 3:23 RSV).

Fortunately, in our recent inflationary spiral, wages have increased, too. However, many families today increase their spending more than their wages. With higher wages propelling them into higher tax brackets, they spend the wage increase without actually checking to see what's left to spend.

With spending often going for new cars or larger houses, the item purchased actually adds to future spending needs, reducing the amount available for basic necessities.

Inflation is certainly changing our life-styles. Several years from now, we'll look back on today as the good old days. We'll remember when we drove large, air-

conditioned cars wherever and whenever we wanted. We'll
remember that most of us owned our own beautiful homes
which were comfort-conditioned year round. We'll remember using cheap water to water our green grass, run
garbage down our disposals, and take long, hot showers.
We'll think fondly of our frequent travels, our charcoal-
broiled steaks, and our frequent meals eaten out.

I've never seen anyone beat inflation with debt. The
people I see in the worst trouble financially, now, in a time
of high employment and rising wages, are those who are
living beyond their means.

We must be ready to adjust our life-styles. If the cost of
air-conditioning our houses goes so high we can't pay for
it, we have some tough choices to make. One is to turn off
the cooling system and suffer with the heat. (The Bible, for
example, has much to say about suffering, most of it relat-
ing to how much we can learn, grow, and depend on the
Lord during our suffering.) Or we can cut out such things
as travel, clothes, life insurance, college educations, recreation, and eating out. Borrowing money to pay for the air
conditioning won't solve the problem. Getting angry at the
utility company won't solve the problem. Demanding
higher wages from our employers won't solve the problem.
The inflation problem can only be solved when the elected
representatives of our cities, states, and nation use the
self-control to say *no* to overspending and *yes* to living
within our means. The inflation problem can only be solved in your household when you say *no* to overspending
and *yes* to living within your means. Someone has said, "It
is not the high cost of living that is our problem, but it is
the cost of living high that is our problem."

Here are some practical things you can do to keep from
being hit by rising costs:

Turn off your air conditioner. The rising utility costs will
not affect you too much, if you eliminate the most costly
item.

Stop eating out. Our eating habits today allow for many more meals out than were normal a few years ago. Since service is a major factor in meals served in restaurants, the price of restaurant meals has increased more rapidly than dining at home.

Make do with what you have. Any item you don't buy keeps you from paying the inflated prices of the new item.

One of my co-workers says she intends to beat inflation by investing in taxes, because each year they keep going up.

The Inflation Mentality

"Buy now! If you don't, the price will be so high, later, that you may never be able to afford it." Such a philosophy was expressed in a poem I heard in college. The theme was marriage, but the subject could be anything else you want now, but don't have the money to buy.

The bride bent with age, leaned over her cane
Her steps uncertain need guiding . . .
While down the church aisle with a wan, toothless smile,
The groom in a wheel chair gliding.

And who is this elderly couple thus wed?
You'll find when you've closely explored it,
That this is that rare, most conservative pair
Who WAITED 'TIL THEY COULD AFFORD IT!

In recent years not many consumers waited till they could afford it.

But, why wait? Won't whatever you buy cost more in the future? Isn't it smart planning to buy now at a lower price and pay back later with dollars made cheaper by inflation?

Two illustrations from my counseling may reveal two opposite approaches to the inflation problem. One couple came to me with debts beyond their current ability to pay.

When they bought their house one year ago, they had no debt. Now they owed $2,400. What had happened? The house they bought to save money cost more than they had planned. Insurance, taxes, and maintenance were all items to which they had closed their eyes when they bought their home. Slowly, each month they sank deeper and deeper into debt.

Solomon described their situation and the reason for their plight: "For you closed your eyes to the facts and did not choose to reverence and trust the Lord. . . . That is why you must eat the bitter fruit of having your own way and experience the full terrors of the pathway you have chosen" (Proverbs 1:29, 31 LB). Can you imagine the trauma they faced as they attempted to reduce spending by the $200 a month they had been overspending and then by another $200 a month to repay the debt?

Investing to Save

It makes no sense to buy something now if the expenses it will add to your budget will cause you to overspend your income. But it does make sense to buy something now if it will lower your expenses now and in the future. If, that is, you can afford the purchase!

An insulation salesman called on me. With my permission he showed me that the insulation in my attic was lacking the recommended R value. By adding R-19 to my ceiling insulation, he estimated that 20% of my gas and electric bills would be saved. In addition, he pointed out that the federal government would allow me a tax credit of 15% of the cost of my insulation. Then he quoted the price of $675 to insulate my attic.

Remembering what Solomon declared: "Only a simpleton believes what he is told! A prudent man checks to see where he is going" (Proverbs 14:15 LB), I decided to gather some more facts. A check with the city energy department confirmed that R-30 was the recommended amount of insulation for my house. Their estimate of utility savings was for 10% instead of 20%. Noting another Proverb, "Plans go wrong with too few counselors; many counselors bring success" (Proverbs 15:22 LB), I sought more counsel. The specialist at the local electric company said experience with their customers proved that 10% electric and gas savings was possible.

My accountant confirmed the tax credit and pointed out what it meant to me. Fifteen percent of the insulation cost was deducted from my next year's taxes due.

Now it was time for the figures:

Cost of insulation	$675
Less tax credit of 15%	101
Net cost	$574

Savings at 10% utility cost, assuming utilities increase 10% per year, are as follows:

Year	Cost	Savings at 10%	Cumulative Savings
1978	$ 875		
1979	963	$ 96	$ 96
1980	1,059	106	202
1981	1,165	116	318
1982	1,282	128	446
1983	1,410	141	587

At the end of five years, my savings amount to more than I invested in the insulation. And *that* seems like a sensible investment that will reap dollar returns to me as long as I live in this house.

In the first illustration, the couple increased their monthly expenses beyond their capacity. The insulation example was an investment that was projected to lower expenses. Which would appear to you to be the prudent investment? Which alternative looks like the best way to beat inflation?

Marjean's 2¢: Investing or Spending?

I often hear someone say, "I invested in a new iron" or a new set of dishes or similar items. Inwardly I smile because of the use of the term *invest*.

Webster's definition of *invest* is "to use (money) to buy something that is expected to produce a profit, or income, or both." I wonder if that person really does intend for that iron or set of dishes to produce a profit or income. Or is he using that word to justify his spending the money? Perhaps he's even buying it on time?

We all need to be careful not to fool ourselves into thinking we are *investing* money, when we are really *spending* it.

---

3 *Preparing for the Car Squeeze*

Solomon, in the Book of Proverbs, contrasts the wise man with the fool. When it comes to facts, he says, "The wise man looks ahead. The fool attempts to fool himself and won't face facts" (Proverbs 14:8 LB). You'd be surprised how many people are fools when it comes to cars. I easily spot people fooling themselves, when they show me their budgets.

Sam was a business executive earning over $36,000 annually. During the past year, since he had moved into his present house, he had accumulated over $6,000 in short-term debts. The budget he and his wife sent me showed spending equal to income. Obviously, you don't go $500 a month in the hole unless you are spending more than you make. Sam's budget evidently had some leaks. Since the investigative techniques of Sherlock Holmes have long been favorites of mine, I was challenged to look for the leaks. Much financial counseling has taught me that the one place to begin is to examine closely the car category of the budget.

Sam's monthly budget figures showed the following under transportation:

Gas	$160
Repairs	30
Insurance	50
Total	$240

My next step was to follow Solomon's advice, "Get the facts at any price, and hold on tightly to all the good sense you can get" (Proverbs 23:23 LB).

I called Sam. "How many cars do you have, Sam?"

"Three," he replied.

"How many miles a month are you driving your cars?" I inquired. (Since his last move was to a house twenty-two miles from his work, five miles from his teenagers' school, and two miles from shopping, I suspected that his family was driving many miles.)

After a quick look at his odometers, Sam was back on the phone. "Three thousand," he said. "But that sounds too high to me."

"Not surprising," I replied. "That's about fourteen hundred miles for your car and eight hundred miles apiece for each of your other cars. Three thousand miles a month sounds right to me for your active family."

Next I took out my calculator and divided the $240 his budget showed for car expense by the 3,000 miles they were driving and arrived at $.08 per mile.

"Can you drive your car for eight cents a mile, Sam?"

"No way," he answered.

Here was one huge hole in Sam's budget. Assuming a conservative $.25 per mile to drive his cars, Sam's spending plan was short by a whopping $510.00 a month ($.25 − $.08 = $.17 × 3,000 miles = $510.00).

Now are *you* ready for these facts? At $.25 per mile, Sam's family was actually spending $750 each month to drive their cars—not the $240 they were budgeting. How about you? Do you have a gaping hole in your budget dike because you are trying to fool yourself on what it costs to drive *your* car?

Here's the chart:

Table 5: Gas-Tank Facts

Gas Cost	Did I Save for Certain Future Expenses?*
$ 5.00	$16.83
6.00	20.22
7.00	23.63
8.00	27.03
9.00	30.43
10.00	33.83
11.00	37.23
12.00	40.45
13.00	43.86
14.00	47.26
15.00	50.66
16.00	54.06
17.00	57.46
18.00	60.86

MPG = Miles Per Gallon
PG = Per Gallon
Example: $\dfrac{\$10.00 \text{ spent for gas}}{\$1.00 \text{ per gallon}} = 10$ gallons

10 gallons × 15 MPG = 150 miles

Cost = $10.00 (gas) + $33.83 (other) = $43.83

$\dfrac{\text{(Cost) } 43.83}{\text{Miles } \quad 150} = \$.292$ per mile

* Includes: Insurance, taxes, maintenance, repairs, car replacement, for a new car driven 10 years at an average of 10,000 miles a year.

Gas-Tank Facts

Most people calculate the cost of gas and insurance and an occasional emergency repair as the cost of driving their car. When I show them the Gas Tank Facts (table 5), they look at me as if I'm trying to exaggerate the figures or put something over on them. How do you feel about these gas-tank facts?

Every time you fill your tank with gas, the dollar amount shown in the left column, you have just as surely spent the amount in the right hand column during the time you burned the gas. For instance, when you put $12 of gas in your tank, did you also put aside $40.45 for those other certain expenses? If not, you will be surprised when they crop up as a budget buster later.

At one seminar, a woman with an unbelieving look on her face raised her hand. "What are those certain future expenses?" she asked. When I answered, "Insurance, taxes, repairs, maintenance, and money to replace this car when you change cars," the unbelieving look continued. She simply said, "Oh." She was just too polite to say, "I don't believe it. It doesn't cost me that much to drive my car. Unless you prove it to me, I just won't believe it, Mr. Fooshee."

She was right. The costs of car ownership are so unbelievable that I need to prove them to myself again and again. So fasten your seat belt and hang on.

Seeing Is Believing

"Twenty-five cents a mile! Absurd. I know we don't spend anywhere near twenty-five cents a mile to drive our cars!" With such unbelief, dozens of counselees have returned from our financial sessions, blindly ignoring true car costs. They continue to fool themselves into believing that they can afford two cars, long weekend trips, cars for their kids, and other such luxuries.

Jesus said to the disciples, "Do you have eyes but fail to see, and ears but fail to hear? . . ." (Mark 8:18 NIV). My goal is to show you so clearly what it costs to drive a car that you'll literally hear the meter ticking every time you make a decision about your car.

Let's make some assumptions:

Car cost	$5,500
Miles driven a year	12,000
Number of years driven	5
Car value when sold	$825
Gas mileage average	15 MPG
Drivers	2 adults

Car Cost Starting with a car costing $5,500 and assuming you will replace it with a $5,500 car five years from now, you will need to save $4,675. Here's the breakdown:

Cost of present car	$5,500
Sell car in five years	825
Cost to replace present car	$4,675

$4,675 ÷ 5 years = $935 per year or $77.91 per month
$4,675 ÷ 60,000 miles = .0779¢ per mile

You will need to set aside $77.91 each month, or $.0779 each mile you drive, to have enough money to replace your car five years from now, or 60,000 miles later.

To give you an idea of what $5,500 will buy at the beginning of 1979, here's your shopping list.

New 1979—Chevy Monza, Chevy Chevette, Ford Pinto Station Wagon

Used 1978—Chrysler Cordoba, Cutlass Supreme, Buick LeSabre V-8, Mercury Marquis

Used 1977—Buick Regal Landau Coupe, Grand Prix, Ford LTD Wagon

Used 1976—Buick Electra, Ford Thunderbird

Used 1975—BMW 2002

Used 1974—Lincoln Mark IV, Porsche 914 Roadster

Our company replaced a salesman's car we had bought used in July 1973. The old car had been driven over 80,000 miles in the 65 months we owned it.

The new (used, of course) car cost us $4,215, including a 3% sales tax after deducting the $600 the old car sold for. Simple math shows that we had to set aside $64.87 each month to have the $4,215 to pay for the new car. Since we drove the old one 80,000 miles, we had to plan on setting aside $.0527 every mile we drove to have enough money to buy the new one.

Had we bought a 1979 model, instead of the 1977 model with 23,000 miles on it, the same model *new* car with the same equipment would have cost us $6,932, or $2,717 more. That's a whopping 64% more than the used car we bought. To buy the new one, we would have needed to set aside $41.80 more each month, for a total of $106.67 each month.

The amount set aside would have needed to be $.034 per mile more, or a total of $.0867 for each mile driven.

An easy way to see our car cost per mile is evident from this chart.

	New Car	Used Car
Projected mileage for car	100,000	100,000
Mileage on used car when purchased		− 23,000
Mileage available on newly purchased car		77,000
Cost of car	$6,932	$4,215
Cost per mile	$.0693	$.0547

The difference in car costs between buying the new car and the used one is $.0146 for each mile driven, *up to* the 100,000 total miles on the car. Do you see why we buy them used?

Gas cost Feeding gas to your 15 MPG guzzler over 12,000 miles means you must buy 800 gallons of gas. At an average price of $1.00 per gallon, you've spent $800.

In case you're driving a real gas miser, you might be doing better.

12,000 miles at	Gallons	Total cost at $1.00 per gallon	Cost per mile
15 MPG	800	$800	$.067
20 MPG	600	600	.05
25 MPG	480	480	.04
30 MPG	400	400	.033

Insurance Insurance rates on the same car vary infinitely and are based on the city, state, company, drivers, car use, make and model, and coverage.

Our assumptions lead us to insure a $5,500 Chevy Impala four-door in Wichita, Kansas, for two adult drivers for business and pleasure purposes. We've used a $100 collision deductible with liability coverage of $100,000–$300,000 and actual, cash-value comprehensive.

Using a premium from a national insurance company, we'll be paying $318 for the first year. Insurance totals $.027 a mile for our 12,000 annual miles.

Interest cost Since over 72% of all cars are purchased with borrowed money, we need to include an interest amount. Most people use their old car, plus a little cash for the down payment. We'll assume that $4,500 will be financed at 14% interest for three years. Interest totals $1,037 and adds $.017 per mile over the 60,000 miles.

Taxes and licenses Taxes also vary widely from location to location. We'll assume you're being taxed both the Kansas personal-property tax and the annual license ȯn the used two-year-old Chevy. Those two figures total $157 in the first year (when the car is two model years old) and will total approximately $602 for the five years we drive the car. And that's another $.01 a mile.

Repairs and maintenance   *Beware!* This category is the trouble spot. People seem to think car repairs are: unusual, emergencies, and bad luck. Not so! They are: common, usual, routine, and necessary.

My present company car is a 1973 Ford with 87,000 miles on the odometer. Counting the oil changes and lubes (every 2,000 to 2,500 miles), it has been in the shop fifteen times in the last twelve months. Let's see what $.06 per mile, $60 per month, or $720 per year will install in your car, at 1979 prices.

2 standard radial tires	$180.00
1 battery	55.00
5 oil changes (with lube and filter)	83.00
2 shocks	40.00
1 brake job	120.00
replace hoses	45.00
1 minor tune-up with six plugs and points	50.00
1 service call to jump battery or change tire	12.00
1 wheel alignment, wheel balancing, and rotating tires	30.00
1 water pump	70.00
1 fuel pump	31.00
Total	$716.00

You may think, "This is absurd. I won't need all those things in any one year." You may be right. But, remember we've left out some others that might add to your costs, such as:

vandalism to the car ($100 deductible)	$60.00
accident ($100 deductible)	100.00
electrical repair	25.00
muffler and tail pipe	100.00
carburetor overhaul	45.00
air-conditioner repair	200.00
heater repair	90.00
two more radials	180.00
alternator	40.00
starter	55.00
transmission replacement	325.00
valve job	225.00

Take your pick. Each of these items in the first list has an average cost of approximately $65. For your $60 per month, or $.06 per mile, you can do eleven of them each year. If you get by for less this year, just wait till next year.

The only way I came to believe these figures myself was to keep a small repair-and-maintenance log book in my glove compartment. That black book made a believer of me. Why don't you try it?

Summary Here are the costs we've figured for our $5,500.00 Chevy.

Total Cost	Per Mile
Car cost	$.078
Gas	.067
Insurance	.027
Interest	.017
Taxes and licenses	.010
Repairs and maintenance	.060
Total	$.259

The ticking meter Our hypothetical car is costing us $.245 each mile. Yours may be costing less, or it may be costing more.

If you are driving a car that costs less than our $5,500 one, your car cost is less. If you average more than 15 MPG, your gas cost is less. If you live where insurance rates are lower than those used, you'll save a little on insurance. If you buy for cash instead of financing, you have no interest cost. But you do lose the interest you would have earned if the cash had been invested in savings instead of spent on a car. If you have a car that seldom needs repairs, or if you do all your own repairs, you'll save some more here.

But my experience is that most families don't buy used cars, do borrow money to pay for them, do drive more than 12,000 miles a year, do have terrific repair bills, and would drool at the low insurance costs I've quoted. And to make the car costs really exciting, they are driving two or more cars, often with teenage drivers who send the insurance, mileage, and repairs to even higher levels.

Are you willing to settle for $.259 a mile? Here's what your costs are:

Miles	Costs Fixed *	Variable Total **	Total	Daily	Monthly
12,000	$.132	$.127	$3,108	$ 8.52	$259.00
15,000	.132	.127	3,885	10.64	324.00
18,000	.132	.127	4,662	12.77	389.00
24,000	.132	.127	6,216	17.03	518.00

*Car cost: depreciation or replacement, insurance, taxes, and interest.

**Gasoline, maintenance and repairs.

Seeing is believing! Buy your cars with your eyes wide open to the real costs. Calculate your own costs of your next car. Then put those costs in your budget. If they fit well, rejoice. If they blow the budget, consider another alternative.

Marjean's 2 ¢:
"These Figures Boggle My Mind!"

These figures boggle my mind!

I am aware that the price of gasoline is going up. My question is, "How can I, a housewife, help ease the pressure my husband feels with continually mounting costs?" First of all, I can be content with what he provides for me. Sure, I'm driving a '63 Chevy, but it gets me every place I need to go. We keep it up by checking the oil, battery, hoses, and radiator water each time I buy gas.

Speaking of "places I need to go," that is the second way I can help cut the costs. My week is planned so that errands and grocery shopping can be limited to one or two days a week. I know when and where I will be on certain days of the week. So such things as dropping off or picking up the cleaning can be done on my way someplace else, instead of making a special trip out for that. I resist, like the plague, the pull to jump in my car to run one errand for a special need.

When the girls were at home with lessons, Girl Scouts, and other activities, I planned my errands around their trips. Encourage your family to help with this. Post an "I need" list on the refrigerator. When anyone runs out of an item, jot it down there. Ultimately incorporate it into your shopping list.

Inform your family of the day you will be out running errands. Then any of their needs can be taken care of at that time. As we "Do nothing from selfishness or conceit, but in humility," we ". . . look not only to [our] . . . own interests, but also to the interests of others" (Philippians 2:3, 4 RSV). We are working together in a family, rather than resenting the demands we feel are put on us. And I feel that I am doing what I can in the area of helping my husband.

Questions

1. If you find the car you own is costing you too much money, what is the best thing to do? Mine is only one year old. The writer of Proverbs had the answer for you, centuries ago:

> You may have trapped yourself by your agreement. Quick! Get out of it if you possibly can! Swallow your pride; don't let embarrassment stand in the way. Go and beg to have your name erased. Don't put it off. Do it now. Don't rest until you do. If you can get out of this trap you have saved yourself like a deer that escapes from a hunter, or a bird from the net.
>
> Proverbs 6:2–5 LB

2. You talk about old cars being economical. A young single woman is thinking about purchasing her first car. Is it practical for her to buy an "old clunker" when she is not a mechanic? There is a lot of difference between a new car and an old clunker, both in price and in age, and most of us who drive cars are not mechanics. My mother is still driving her eighteen-year-old Ford, which causes her no more trouble than some of the new cars a few of her friends drive. There's also a lot of difference in price between a new car and a two- or three-year-old car, but not that much difference in utility.

3. If you can afford to buy new cars, is it wrong to drive nice cars, have nice clothes, and other luxuries, especially if you are tithing? The real question concerns whether you have the nice cars, clothes, and things or whether these things have you. Do you love to give or do you love to get?

Faithful tithing is not automatic license for you to buy whatever you want. In our own situation, the way the Lord has blessed us, a tithe would be stingy. Our own giving goal is to have our giving exceed our living expenses. To do this, we must do without many of the "nice things we want." For Marjean and me, part of that doing without has included new cars.

4. In a business, do you recommend leasing a new car? My own company buys used cars. If you lease a car, you're paying for a new one, plus interest on the money, plus a profit for the leasing company. We buy two- to three-year-old cars with 20,000 to 30,000 miles on them, so we save the interest and leasing company's profit, as well as the difference between the price of the new car and the price of the used one.

5. How do you know how much to figure for transportation per mile? The best way is to gather your own figures. Earlier in this chapter, I gave you the outline and guidelines. This is really an important question. My experience has proved that few people plan to spend what it really costs to run their car(s).

One day I was speaking in an upper-level business class in a Christian college. For starters, I asked how many of the twelve students had cars there at college. Ten students replied affirmatively.

Next I asked them to tell me how much a month it was costing them to drive their cars. Silence!

As I went to the chalkboard, I began to ask them some questions. I discovered they were driving everything from an old clunker to a $10,000 'vette.

When we had finished, they had proved to me and to themselves that it was costing them an average of $150 per month to drive each of those cars. And they didn't even know it!

6. What's the best way to buy a used car? Decide how you will use the car. Decide what size and what kind of car will meet those needs. Decide how much money you want to spend. Read the latest annual auto issue of *Consumer Reports,* which usually comes out in April. You may get it from your local library or subscribe to it directly (Orangeburg, New York 10962). Study it carefully. Decide what make, model, and year of car will meet your needs. Pray for the Lord to supply the exact car to meet your needs. Then do as He leads you.

When we look for a new car for our company salesmen, we ask God to provide a two-year-old model of a Ford or Chevrolet, with the best repair record, with less than 30,000 miles on it, with one owner with whom we can talk, and for a selling price that is at least 35% below a new car of the same make. And He always has.

4 Revealing the House Squeeze: It's Outasight!

At lunch one day, Jerry, a young attorney, asked, "How much should I save before I can buy a house?"

"That's a good question," I replied.

After thinking about it a minute, I said, "About seven thousand dollars. That will give you a four thousand dollar down payment on a forty-thousand-dollar house, one thousand five hundred closing and moving costs, and one thousand five hundred dollars left over for emergencies."

I soon discovered that was a bad answer.

Look what could have happened to Jerry if he'd taken my off-the-cuff answer seriously:

	Monthly	Annually
House cost		$40,000
Down payment		$4,000
Mortgage: (30 years at 10¾%)		$36,000
Mortgage payment	$336.05	$4,033
Insurance (.5% of the cost)	$16.67	$200
Taxes (2.5% of the cost)	$83.33	$1,000
Maintenance (2% of the cost)	$66.66	$800
Utilities (3% of the cost)	$100.00	$1,200
Totals	$602.72	$7,233

Jerry's projected gross income for 1979 is $18,000, or $1,500 monthly.

Here's what the shelter expenses look like, compared to his income:

$$\frac{\text{Monthly Expense } \$603}{\text{Monthly Income } \$1,500} = 40.2\% \qquad \frac{\text{Annual Expense } \$7,233}{\text{Annual Income } \$18,000} = 40.2\%$$

You try balancing your budget after paying out 40.2% of all your gross income for the place where you live. If you succeed, write me and let me know how you did it.

Realtors used to tell people that they could buy a house that cost two and one-half times their annual gross income. Recently I've read articles suggesting that your monthly house payment can total 25% of your gross income.

What are the rules of thumb? Should I tell Jerry to buy what he *wants* in a house? Or should I figure out what Jerry *can afford* to buy? Maybe I need to ask myself, "How much house can Jerry afford to buy?"

Be prepared for a shock!

Housing: It's Outasight!

Time magazine's September 12, 1977, cover story was on sky-high housing. The article was entitled "Housing: It's Outasight."

Since 1970, the median price of a new house shot up from $23,386 to an unbelievable $64,700 at the beginning of 1979. That's an increase of $41,314—up 177%.

Outasight!

Based on the median family income of $9,867 in 1970, approximately one-half of American families could qualify for the purchase of a $23,386 new home. In those days the rule of thumb was that you could buy a home costing two and one-half times your annual income (2.5 × $9,867 gross annual income = $24,668 cost of home).

Since 1970, almost all costs associated with home ownership have increased. Home-mortgage interest rates are up from 8.5% to at least 10.75% in late 1979. Taxes, insurance, utilities, and maintenance have also skyrocketed.

My own rule of thumb for a house purchase is that you *may* afford a house not to exceed 1.7 times your annual gross family income.

If you buy a house costing this amount:	Your annual gross earnings will need to be at least:
$20,000	$11,764
25,000	14,705
30,000	17,647
35,000	20,588
40,000	23,529
45,000	26,470
50,000	29,411
55,000	32,352
60,000	35,294
70,000	41,176
80,000	47,059
90,000	52,941
100,000	58,823
120,000	70,588
140,000	82,352
160,000	94,117
200,000	117,647

Outasight!

Such figures are so far "outasight" that large numbers of people are refusing to believe them. Instead, they listen to the realtors' smooth pitch to "bite the bullet." "You'll never be able to buy this cheaply again," they say, and "You'll be making four to six hundred dollars a month while you live here." And they "bite the bullet." They reason that the payment is just a few dollars more than their present payment. And it will be a super investment. And they will cut someplace else.

Most families I've counseled this year have increased their family debt by $150 to $500 a month from the time they bought their house until the time they sought help for their financial problems.

Outasight!

That's right! *Outasight* because they didn't look to see what was involved beyond that monthly house payment. Let's look at those figures and hear them speak.

Marjean's 2¢: The House That's "Just Perfect"

"But this house is just *perfect* for us!" This is the cry we hear when George shows the couple the facts about the figures on the house they want to buy. (If they haven't already bought it!)

I shudder when I remember the house I thought was "just perfect" for us. We had been engaging in the Sunday-afternoon sport of touring open houses for sale. There was a house not far from ours—same school district, grocery stores, and friends. We loved it. Oh, there were a few minor problems with it, but we could overlook them.

The asking price was more than George was willing to pay, but he made an offer. In the time that lapsed before we heard from the owner, I had mentally moved into the house, arranged our furniture in each of the rooms, decided which bedrooms would be occupied by whom, and entertained our first guests. Would you believe that when the owner turned down our offer, George refused to go up? I was *crushed*. After all, it was "just perfect" for us.

How thankful I am now that George got the facts and stuck to them, despite my pleas, and that we waited on God's house, which truly is "just perfect" for us.

The Shocking Truth

My friend's income of $18,000 a year means that he will have to struggle to pay for a $30,000 house and balance his budget at the same time. Here's the way I wrote out the estimates for him:

Cost of house		$30,000
Down payment (10%)		3,000
Mortgage (30 years at 10¾%)		$27,000
	Monthly	Annually
Mortgage payment	$252.04	$3,024.48
Insurance (.5%)	12.50	150.00
Taxes (2.5%)	62.50	750.00
Maintenance (2%)	50.00	600.00
Utilities (4%)	100.00	1,200.00
Total	$477.04	$5,724.48

The best rule of thumb I've seen is that all expenses for the place where you live should not exceed 30% of your total gross income.

Thirty percent of Jerry's $18,000 income is $5,400. His housing costs will exceed the maximum allowable by $324.48 annually.

His alternatives are: buy a $28,000 house with a $3,000 down payment. Expenses on the same formula total $5,321, slightly below the $5,400 rule of thumb. Or if he paid $2,000 more down, bringing his down payment to $5,000, his mortgage on a $30,000 house would be reduced to $25,000, which would lower his monthly payment by $18.66, or $223.92 a year. His total annual cost would be $5,500, very close to the $5,400 maximum.

The assumption is that you make only a 10% down payment. Here are two houses with expenses worked out to show you what you'll need to operate some higher-priced homes:

	Monthly	Annually
Cost of house		$70,000
Down payment (10%)		7,000
Mortgage (30 years at 10¾%)		$63,000
Mortgage payment	$ 588.10	$7,057.20
Insurance (.5%)	29.17	350.00
Taxes (2.5%)	145.83	1,750.00
Maintenance (2%)	116.66	1,400.00
Utilities (4%)	233.33	2,800.00
Total	$1,113.09	$13,357.20

The gross income necessary to support this house is $41,176 per year, or $3,431 monthly. The $1,113.09 monthly cost is 32.4% of gross income. Families with higher incomes often choose to spend a higher percentage of those incomes for housing.

	Monthly	Annually
Cost of house		$120,000
Down payment (10%)		12,000
Mortgage (30 years at 10¾%)		$108,000
Mortgage payment	$1,008.17	$12,098.04
Insurance (.5%)	50.00	600.00
Taxes (2.5%)	250.00	3,000.00
Maintenance (2%)	200.00	2,400.00
Utilities (4%)	400.00	4,800.00
Total	$1,908.17	$22,898.04

The gross income necessary to support this house is $70,588 per year, or $5,882 monthly. The $1,908.17 monthly cost is 32.4% of gross income.

One young man said to me recently, "I thought shelter expense meant only the house payment." A young lady was proudly showing pictures of their new home to a friend. She said, "In a few months we'll find out if we can afford it." Rules of thumb are just that—guidelines and measuring sticks. Your own figures may check out higher or lower. But, *get the facts!* After you've moved into your new home is too late to find out you can't afford it.

Use this guide to figure your own potential housing costs:

Cost of house	_____
Less down payment	_____
Mortgage	_____

	Monthly	Annually
Monthly payment	_____	_____
Insurance (.5%)	_____	_____
Taxes (2.5%)	_____	_____
Maintenance (2%)	_____	_____
Utilities (4%)	_____	_____
Total	_____	_____

Use the monthly payment schedule for mortgage interest amounts from the following:

Monthly Payment for 30 years at:	Per $1,000 of Mortgage:
9.00%	$8.05
9.50%	8.41
9.75%	8.60
10.00%	8.78
10.25%	8.97
10.50%	9.15
10.75%	9.34
11.00%	9.53
11.25%	9.72
11.50%	9.91

Some comments will be helpful on the expense estimates. Insurance on your home will depend on many factors. Location, type of construction, age of house, size of house, types of coverage, deductibles—each will affect what you pay. The best way is to get estimates from two or three insurance agents. Taxes also vary according to city, state, rates, Proposition 13, and a host of other factors. Maintenance—maintenance—maintenance: Doesn't it sound absurd to budget 2% of the cost of your home for annual maintenance? If you own your own home now, go back and look at your check stubs for four years. If your house has averaged $50,000 in market value, at 2% of the value of your house each year, you would have spent $4,000 in four years, for all maintenance. Here are some of the items that aren't included in the house payment, insurance, taxes, or utility categories, which you may have to count on in the maintenance category:

Repairs on:	Purchase of or Replacement of:
Furnace	Furnace
Air conditioner	Air conditioner
Plumbing	Water tank
Sewers	Wiring
Lights and wiring	Oven
Oven	Disposal
Burners	Refrigerator
Disposal	Freezer
Refrigerator	Washer
Freezer	Dryer
Doors	Water softener
Windows	Small appliances
Washer	Dishwasher
Dryer	Dishes
Small appliances	Linens
Dishwasher	Mattresses
Sidewalks	Furniture
Driveways	Carpet

Repairs on:	Purchase of or Replacement of:
Siding	Floor coverings
Roof	Roof
Water softener	Trees
Cleaning, painting, or	Shrubs and flowers
maintenance inside	Sidewalks
house and outside	Driveways
house	Fences
Carpets	
Floors	
Insect or termite control	
Insulation	

In addition to those, you have outside expenses:

Yard care
Fertilizer
Mowing
Spraying
Edging
Snow removal
Tree care

Your list may not include all the things on my list. Great! Scratch them off. However, you may have special items that aren't on my list.

A homeowner faces constant surprises. One day I heard what sounded like running water coming from my basement. Investigation proved that my water tank had sprung a leak. Solutions: use cold water or buy a new tank.

My roof was shot. Alternatives: leaks in my house or buy a new roof. Would you believe that wood shingles on my roof cost $4,500 in May of 1976! And in March of 1979 the cost for that same roof is $6,200.

The shocking truth is that it costs money to own your own home.

Marjean's 2¢: The Shocking Truth

That list of possible repairs or replacements *is* shocking!

What if they all needed repair at once? You can't plan for that in your maintenance, can you? No, but you can learn to wait on some repairs, until you can plan for them.

"But how can I wait, when my dishwasher has broken down?" Just as some friends of ours did. They enlisted the troops and had some good talk time, while washing and drying dishes. The same family's disposal broke down. They learned to wrap garbage in old newspapers and carry it to the trash. Then the ultimate: No family of six can do without a washing machine, but they did, when theirs went on the blink. They just did not have the cash to repair or replace all those items at once, so they went to the Laundromat. My friend reported that at least two of the family members went to the laundry each time, and they had some great conversations.

For "We know that in everything God works for good with those who love him, who are called according to his purpose" (Romans 8:28 RSV). His purpose is for us to trust Him and wait, instead of plunging ahead to spend money we do not have.

Questions

The housing area has produced the most questions by seminar participants. The most-often-asked question concerns whether a home mortgage violates the scriptural principle of keeping out of debt. The answer is found in this chapter on housing, which shows the difference between overspending and making a well-planned monthly payment that fits within your budget. Overspending results in debt. The house payment results in building an equity in your home, which becomes an asset—just the opposite of debt.

Other questions not answered in the chapter have been included here.

1. What about going into debt for a house, as against renting an apartment?   In my book *You Can Be Financially Free*, in answering the question of whether it was better to rent or buy, I gave a crisp, "It all depends." You'll have to weigh all the factors, seek the Lord's direction, then act.

Here's an illustration that will help you calculate your own situation. A friend of mine and his wife rent a nice two-bedroom house for $160, an unheard-of rent, at this time, in our town. The house came as the result of specific prayer. Since they are renting, their only additional shelter expenses are for utilities, which are averaging $70, making the total expenses $230 a month. What can they buy?

With a house payment only making up about 60% of shelter costs, their house payment could total $138 a month for principal and interest (60% of the $230 they spend now). Such a payment will support a 30-year, 10¾% mortgage of approximately $14,800. With a down payment of $1,600 added to the mortgage, the house they could buy for their present expenses could cost $16,400. Since the house they live in is valued at $20,000, they couldn't afford to buy it, unless they could increase their budget for housing by $48 a month, or increase their down payment by $3,600.

By continuing to rent, they'll accumulate the difference between the rent they pay and the amount they can save through not having higher housing costs. They'll also not have to fix the leaky roof, the crumbling foundation, or paint the outside of the house.

By buying, if the house appreciates, they'll accumulate the equity they build as the mortgage is reduced *and* the additional amount the house may sell for several years later. As they invest time in fixing up the house, they'll add additional value which may be gained when they sell.

If the past trend of inflation on real-estate property continues, the house purchase should work out to be the better plan. They should pray over such a decision and seek counsel from others.

2. *What about debts for houses?* This decision will depend on your goals. Many Christians today have the long-term goal of becoming debt free to the glory of God.

Long-term financial planning should certainly include a debt-free home. In our own case we applied some of our annual savings to our mortgage payment. Since each annual additional payment applied to the principal only, each extra annual payment reduced, by over two years, the number of years we had left to pay. It was a lot of fun to cross out those payments on that long chart and to have the mortgage paid off in half the time.

Savings money paid on your mortgage is not readily available, except at great cost and inconvenience. I'd seldom recommend that anyone put *all* their savings into paying off their home loan. But if you are saving regularly, and if your long-term goal is to have a mortgage-free house, then a regular, annual, additional loan payment will greatly reduce the length of your mortgage.

Beware! Some loans contain a penalty provision for prepayment. You may be penalized for additional payments or for payments beyond a certain percentage of your loan. Check this provision before you sign any home loan or before you attempt prepayment.

3. *I cosigned a note on a house for my daughter and her husband. So far there has been no problem; however, how*

can I get out of this? My daughter is a strong Christian, and I am the one who encouraged them to buy a house. Your counsel and your motives for your daughter and her husband seem in their best interest. However, the cosigning violated two scriptural principles: the prohibitions against cosigning in Proverbs 17:18 and the leave-and-cleave principle found in Matthew 19:5. "It is poor judgment to countersign another's note, to become responsible for his debts" (Proverbs 17:18 LB). ". . . For this reason a man shall leave his father and mother and be joined to his wife, and the two shall become one . . ." (Matthew 19:5 RSV).

Since the mortgage needed a cosigner, the lender did not feel that your daughter and her husband could handle the house. It is your financial condition that has allowed them to buy more house than they could afford.

A pastor in financial trouble came to me for counsel. When he came to the pastorate, the church loaned him an interest-free down payment so that he could buy far more house than he could afford. Several months later, his overspending had caught up with him, and he faced severe financial problems.

Possibly your daughter and her husband are in better financial condition now than when they bought the house (I surely hope they aren't in worse financial shape). The lender might now consider allowing your name to be withdrawn. It's worth a try.

5 *Budgeting Helps Unsqueeze Us*

Roger and Debbie had $20 in the bank, no savings, and last month's house payment three weeks past due. Even with both of them working, their next two paychecks would not stretch far enough to pay two house payments, overdue utility bills, food to eat, and gas for the car.

They panicked, and Debbie called me for an appointment.

Their financial summary may shock you, but it was no surprise to me. I've counseled dozens of young couples who are both working and who have messes like this.

Everyone who comes to me for financial counseling must fill out a financial summary before I begin helping them. Roger and Debbie's is shown in table 6.

With thirty-two months of marriage behind them, two good jobs, a $30,500 house in their name, and driving only one small, not-so-new car between them, you'd think they would be in excellent financial shape. Not so! Otherwise, they wouldn't be in my office seeking help.

Table 6: Financial Summary

Date_____

A. What We Own (assets):

1. Money in the bank	$ 20.00	
2. Cash value of life insurance (call agent on each policy)	_____	
3. Savings (savings & loan, credit union, and so forth)	_____	
4. Stocks and bonds (present market value)	_____	
5. Real estate		
a. Home (price home would readily sell for on today's market)	30,500.00	
b. Other real estate	_____	
6. Other investments	_____	
7. Personal possessions (for each room you have that is nicely furnished, multiply by $500)	1,000.00	
8. Automobiles (call car dealer and ask for average retail price of your car/cars)	2,500.00	
9. Other property (boats, trailers, cabins, and so forth)	_____	
10. Special property (cameras, guns, hobbies, motorcycles, silver, camping equipment, stereo equipment)	_____	
11. Interest in retirement or pension plan	_____	

What We Own Totals		
(1–4) Cash & other savings		20.00
(5) Real estate		30,500.00
(6–11) Other property		3,500.00
Grand Total of What We Own		$34,020.00

B. What We Owe	Amounts Due	Monthly Payment	Est. Annual Interest
1. To the mortgager of our home	$24,590	$ 244.00	9%
2. To others	300	25.00	18%
a. Bank	1,250	71.24	12%
b. Loan company	1,335	53.00	28%
c. Credit union	2,450	100.00	12%
d. Insurance companies	0	34.25	?
3. Credit-card companies	750	48.00	18%
4. Other businesses	60	11.00	18%
5. Other—school loan	2,700	35.00	7%
6. Medical or dental	576		____
Grand Total of What We Owe	$34,011	$ 621.49	

A Panicky Present

I started with the usual question, "What is your problem?"

Roger answered, "I think we have too much debt, but I don't think we have more than anybody else."

"What have you done about your problem?" I asked.

"Well, we've prayed about it and talked a lot about it," Roger replied.

A Planless Past

So I asked them the same question I've asked every couple and person who has come to me for financial counsel: "Do you have a written plan for your spending? Do you have a budget?"

And I heard the same answer I've always heard, "No." (The only deviation from that blunt answer has been the occasional couple who says, "We tried that once, but it didn't work.")

I started adding up the debt figures they had brought in on the financial summary. The total came to $9,421, not counting the $24,590 house mortgage.

Then I told them I was subtracting the $2,700 they brought to the marriage in school loans and the $1,250 her father had loaned them to help with the down payment on their house. The new total of $5,471 of debt was the amount they had overspent their income during their thirty-two months of marriage.

They could hardly believe that they'd overspent by $171 a month. It didn't help much when I told them, "A panicky present is the result of a planless past. Your planless past has caught up with you. Without records and with credit cards, it has been very easy for you to plunge into the debt trap. But it won't be as easy to escape."

Roger and Debbie did what came naturally. Roger was

right: They probably weren't any more in debt than most couples their age who didn't determine, at marriage, to keep out of debt and to keep records.

Over half the couples interviewed in a national survey sponsored by General Mills in 1974 admitted that they fought about money.

One little fellow was asked in Sunday school if he knew the definition of a *budget*. He said, "Yeah, I know what that is: It's a family argument." Marjean and I have found just the opposite. With a plan for our spending that includes room for car and household repairs, that counts on taxes and insurance, and that allows for some vacation time together as a family, we haven't faced the panicky present.

Oftentimes an unexpected financial problem leads us to

the budget book, to look at the facts together. We find what we can do without, what we can say *no* to in order to say *yes* to the present emergency. It is a matter of prayer and of choice between alternatives.

With no spending plan, the choices are not clear. In the maze of confusion, most couples argue about what to do, and then just charge the problem. The increased payments and interest lead to more financial pressures and more frequent arguments.

If you are like the loser Ziggy and believe in living life one lump at a time (*see* figure 1), be prepared for the money battles. If you want to take God's narrow way, read on about the profit of prevention.

Pity the Poor Planner

Over Labor Day weekend in 1978, a group of Christian authors met together in Atlanta. Each had a ministry to the Body of Christ in biblical money management. Each man expresses his emphasis on family financial planning in a different way. Each details the troubles families face when they are poor planners. And each exhorts the readers to face the facts of keeping a spending plan. Let's have them speak for themselves.

Waldo J. Werning is the director of development and a teacher at Concordia Theological Seminary, Fort Wayne, Indiana. He is the author of several books and articles about stewardship. In his *Where Does the Money Go?* he says:

> Budgeting is selecting a standard of living through careful planning to keep within our income. It is a statement of what we believe and also a statement of how much we believe in what we believe . . . .
>
> A suitable spending plan or budget can encourage the accomplishment of many things as a person makes

choices. It frees in spending rather than binds, stimulates rather than depresses. It helps to solve financial problems. It rewards good thinking, wise action, and aids in the attainment of important goals. A good budget tends to eliminate family arguments about finances. The unemotional rules of elementary arithmetic often calm what otherwise might lead to heated discussions.

Budgets can provide an intelligent control over family finances and should result in the most satisfactory use of income. Some mistakenly feel that a budget results in a narrow life, hemmed in by restrictions. But a good budget actually makes possible the attainment of possessions which otherwise would be impossible . . . .

Careful budgeting encourages freedom from financial worry by providing a "pay as you go" method of living . . . .

One of the reasons why you will want to adopt a budget is that unplanned spending makes for *careless* spending. The budget encourages you to keep from spending money you do not have. It will discourage you from buying what you do not need.

George L. Ford is the president of Stewardship Evangelism Foundation, Winona Lake, Indiana. The purpose of the foundation is to conduct stewardship seminars and workshops in churches, seminaries, and colleges. In *All the Money You Need,* Dr. Ford speaks about budgeting.

When you start to talk about budgets, some people want to run away and hide. They think budgets are burdens that take the fun out of life. They see a budget book as a strait jacket that restricts your life and makes a miserable miser of you.

But budgets don't have to be like that. A budget properly used won't enslave you; it will set you free. It doesn't take money away from you; it gives you more money to use for what you want. And since it involves keeping an accurate record, it helps you know where you stand and what progress you're making toward your goals.

Larry Burkett is the director of Christian Financial Concepts in Norcross, Georgia. It is a nonprofit, nondenominational Christian organization, established to teach God's principles of finance. Larry is the author of several books and many articles and pamphlets about scriptural money management. These comments are from his *Your Finances in Changing Times.*

> And yet, few Christians seem to understand the devastation generated through the misuse of money. There are those who have accepted God's financial plan as their own and stand out like giants among their brothers. But, more common is the Christian who withholds this area of his life from God and struggles within the world's financial system. The same frustrations, worries and anxieties which characterize the non-believer are common to many, perhaps most, Christians.
>
> Without a large scale return to God's plan for making, spending and sharing wealth, I fear the same disaster which has overtaken the non-believing world will befall Christians. Outside of God's will we have no immunity to Satan's schemes. Yet we leave ourselves vulnerable to his blows in the realm of finances . . . .
>
> How can anyone manage a home without coordinating income and expenses? As I mentioned earlier, we all have the knack of adjusting expenses to exceed income.

Malcolm MacGregor, a C.P.A., is an author of books about Christian money management, and a leader of seminars about money matters. This quote is from his book *Your Money Matters.*

The startling fact is that if you are not operating on a budget, you are wasting between $50 and $175 a month, depending on how much your income is and at what level you are spending.

George M. Bowman is the executive editor of *The Shantyman,* a Christian paper which takes the Gospel, in story form, to thousands of workers, convicts, seamen, miners, lumberjacks, and Indians. He is an active, free-lance writer and the author of several books on money management. He has served as a financial consultant and manager for Investors Group. The following quote is from his book *How to Succeed With Your Money.*

In order to be a leader one needs to be optimistic. He must have a good outlook for the future. He must be filled with enthusiasm for the things that are to come in the future. Optimism is a needed attitude in a free economy.

Tell me, what could make a man more optimistic than a personal financial program that eliminates debt, worry, and despair, and builds hope and individual security for today and tomorrow? . . .

It is impossible to succeed with our money if we are intent on spending first before we save. The process of spending is a process without an ending. There is always—repeat, always—a place to spend money. If you purchase a home, you can spend money on improvements until your dying day.

The same holds true in any area of spending. For example, with no control on a family food budget, you could spend literally hundreds of dollars a week in that area alone. In the process of spending, money seems to leak through our hands like water from a constantly dripping faucet. And, like a dripping faucet, it is the major cause of a large portion of our incomes going down the drain. It is the constant dribbling that does it. A faucet that drips only one drop per second will run off two hundred gallons of water in one month! And the spending process that dribbles away a penny here and a penny there will run off substantial sums of money over a year . . . .

The cause of overspending is lack of budgetary control. Therefore, the only way to plug those leaks is to exercise controlled spending. Uncontrolled spending can cause such chaos in our lives that we should take a few minutes to discuss just how serious that problem is. The Bible has many illustrations of the results of overspending, but the most complete one is Christ's parable of the younger son in Luke 15. This parable is a picture of the unhappiness experienced by a man lost in sin and of the joy in heaven when such a man returns to his Creator. But it can also be used to show the results of uncontrolled spending.

Amy Ross Young is assistant to the president of Baptist Publications and Accent Books. Her experience and expertise in budget management, inventory control, and cost analysis give her a background knowledge of finances on the business level. In her book, *It Only Hurts Between Paydays,* she writes:

A young couple with opposing purposes in life, an inability to communicate, and a failure to exercise self-discipline in their personal finances—is headed for trouble. If they separate, money problems will be blamed.

On the other hand, a young couple with a common goal, who can discuss their problems, and who know how to control their personal finances, can face the most devastating money crisis—together—and come out on top.

When the almighty dollar causes problems in your marriage, you can fight and run—or, you can stand together and fight your way out. It is your choice.

Dale E. Galloway, pastor of New Hope Community Church in Portland, Oregon, is the author of several books. These comments are from his book, *There Is a Solution to Your Money Problems:*

Multitudes of people are sinking financially simply because they have no financial blueprint. Would you contract with a builder who was known for not using blueprints to build you a new home? If you did, it would be like throwing your money away, and you are a whole lot smarter than that! And yet, many of us keep throwing our money away simply because we have no pattern or plan by which we manage our money . . . .

It is a greater miracle drug than penicillin! It is something that everybody who handles money desperately needs to take, but which no one wants to swallow. What is this miracle drug, this bitter pill that has proven repeatedly to be the miracle-cure medicine for common money ills? *It is called a budget!*

But the truth is that the majority of people do not get into financial trouble by accident; they get there by default, by failing to plan ahead for inevitable unseen expenses.

Bill King, a C.P.A. in Seattle, Washington, is a financial consultant for Boeing Computer Services. Bill also counsels individuals and families in financial matters. What follows is from his book, *Money Talks—It Says Good-By.*

Financial problems do not continue forever. They are either solved or some change comes that alters the situation. To the family who is struggling today I say, "Take heart." With a good financial plan and a few right choices you can end your financial woes. In fact, I would go so far as to say the time is coming where you will look back on your present situation and thank God for the lessons learned while you were there.

Milo Kauffman was president of Hesston College in Hesston, Kansas, from 1932 to 1951. He has spoken, all over the world, for the Mennonite Board of Missions, on the subject of stewardship. His book, *Stewards of God*, contains these words.

> Money! Money! What a phenomenon! What a paradox!
>
> Money is a joy to the steward, a friend of the needy, a grace to the giver, a helper to the servant. It is a great blessing to man.
>
> Money is a snare to the covetous, an evil to the miser, an enemy of the spendthrift, the master of the lover of money. It is a great curse to man.
>
> Money can serve man or rule him. Money can be a blessing or a curse, can enrich or impoverish man, can be man's friend or his enemy, can improve man or ruin him, can mean treasures in heaven or it can mean perdition, can enhance personality or shrivel it, can make man or break him. Money can mean life or it can mean death.

Roger and Debbie were at that crossroads. They had gone with the many and chosen the easy way and wide gate to free spending with easy credit. They can continue in this way and expect to reap more of what they've sown: interest, repayments, money pressures, and arguments, with a high probability of a destroyed marriage. Their joy will be lost. Their witness for Christ will be no more. Or they can decide to enter the hard way and the narrow gate. This trail involves paying for what they buy, when they purchase it. Their debts will be methodically paid off to the glory of God. They'll begin tithing again. They'll do without, and be blessed by the Lord as they walk with Him. The tool, besides prayer and the power of the Holy Spirit, will be a budget.

As the above authors have said, there's profit in planning and problems in procrastination. So let's get with it!

6 *Budgeting: The Way to Unsqueeze*

Of all the definitions of a budget, which I've seen, I still favor the one I've used for years: "planned spending." To supplement my definition, I like the one Jim Underwood of the National Institute of Christian Financial Planning uses: "A budget is telling your money where you want it to go, rather than wondering where it went."

My observation is that most people spend vast amounts of time wondering where it all went. They seem to think that it disappeared into thin air. It didn't, of course. Each coin, bill, and check passed through their hands when they were fully conscious and in possession of all their faculties.

The Priceless Prescription for Preservation

You need to take three steps to establish and maintain your budget.

1. Plan your spending. Fill out the Our Financial Goals sheet (table 6). Make estimates of what you need and want to spend in each category. If the spending is monthly, multiply by twelve to get the annual figure; if the spending is yearly, divide by twelve to get the monthly amount.

Use the Notes for Our Financial Goals to stimulate your thinking in each area. Review the last twelve months' check stubs to get the amounts you spent for the items listed. Enter a monthly amount for any additional category you have (items 19–21). Whatever extras you cannot afford, such as a vacation, leave out.

List all debt payments, excluding the car payment and the house mortgage payment, under debt reduction. Include the house payment under "shelter" and the car payment under "transportation."

Table 7: Our Financial Goals

	Monthly	Annually
1. Tithes and offerings	_____	_____
2. Federal income tax	_____	_____
3. State income tax	_____	_____
4. Social Security tax	_____	_____
5. Other taxes (such as city)	_____	_____
6. Shelter	_____	_____
7. Food	_____	_____
8. Clothing	_____	_____
9. Health	_____	_____
10. Education	_____	_____
11. Life insurance	_____	_____
12. Gifts	_____	_____
13. Transportation	_____	_____
14. Personal allowances	_____	_____
15. Vacations	_____	_____
16. Savings	_____	_____
17. Household purchases	_____	_____
18. Debt reduction	_____	_____
19.	_____	_____
20.	_____	_____
21.	_____	_____
Totals	=========	=========

Notes for Our Financial Goals

These explanations of each category will guide you in arriving at amounts for each spending category. Start with number one and work through them in order. Remember that a journey of 1,000 miles begins with the first step.

1. *Tithes and offerings:* all charitable giving—church, United Way, and so forth.
2. *Federal income tax:* all amounts withheld, estimates paid, and any amounts due with tax return.
3. *State income tax:* all amounts withheld, estimates paid, and any amounts due with tax return.
4. *Social Security tax:* (1979 figures are 6.13% of your first $22,900 earned, maximum for the year is $1,404; same for your spouse; 8.1% if you are self-employed. Nineteen eighty figures are 6.13% of your first $25,900; maximum for the year is $1,588.
5. *Other taxes:* taxes on your wages, such as city income taxes.
6. *Shelter:* (a) If renting, include rent, heat, lights, telephone, household supplies, appliance repairs, magazine and newspaper subscriptions, and other home-related expenses. (b) If buying, include house payments, interest, insurance, real-estate taxes, repairs and maintenance, and other items listed under renting.
7. *Food:* grocery-store items, paper goods, cleaning supplies, pet foods. Include all eating out and carry-out items and school lunches. It may also include entertainment.
8. *Clothing:* purchases, cleaning, repairs. This may be divided with a separate budget for each family member.
9. *Health:* health-insurance premiums, medical, dental, hospital expenses, drug items, medicines, and cosmetics.

10. *Education:* school supplies, books, lessons, college expenses, uniforms, and equipment.
11. *Life insurance:* all premiums, whether paid monthly, quarterly, or annually.
12. *Gifts:* birthdays, anniversaries, special occasions, Christmas, weddings, funerals, office collections, and dues for organizations.
13. *Transportation:* gas, oil, repairs, licenses, personal-property tax, and insurance. Include car payments or an amount set aside to purchase your next car.
14. *Personal allowances:* for each family member to spend personally—hair care, recreation, baby-sitting, hobbies, and children's allowances.
15. *Vacations:* trips, camps, and week-end outings; trips for weddings, funerals, and family visits.
16. *Savings:* amounts set aside, now, for future needs.
17. *Household purchases:* major appliances, furniture, carpeting, and major home maintenance such as roofing and painting.
18. *Debt reduction:* all payments on debt not included in other categories such as: school loans and amounts due relatives, banks, or others.
19–21. *Special categories:* anything tailored to your own needs or desires; these may include a boat, cabin, airplane, or hobby

2. Balance your budget. When you add up your spending plan, you'll be most unusual if the total amount you plan to spend does not exceed your income. The spending usually comes to $100 to $200 each month *above* the net income.

You've just discovered what most people don't learn until it is too late. You've seen in black and white that if you spend the minimum you think it will take you to live, you'll be going into debt every month by $100 to $200. That's the easy way it happens to most folks.

One of my friends used to think that a budget was a way of showing him that he couldn't live on what he made. Now he realizes that a budget is to help him be able to live on what he makes.

Do you know any way you can be more personally involved in your own life than to try to balance a budget that is $100 to $200 out of whack? Communication between husband and wife must be practically forced; choices must be dealt with; involvement in your lives is assured, as you work out the realities of your spending plan. You'll have to cut, trim, shrink, slice, shave, reduce, curtail, and carve dollars everywhere, to reduce that spending.

But, as a Christian, you have hope. So pray now. Ask the Lord to open your eyes and heart to His leading. He wants to meet your *needs.* Jesus gave you a tremendous promise: "What is impossible with men is possible with God" (Luke 18:27 rsv).

Now open your eyes and look at your financial goals again. Start asking questions such as these:

- *Shelter:* Can we afford this place?
- *Food:* Is eating out eating up our food budget? How much money a month could we save with weekly menu planning?
- *Clothing:* Have we prayed specifically for all needs to be met with bargains? Have we explored the good used-clothing stores and tried the garage sales in expensive neighborhoods?
- *Health:* Would regular exercise cut our doctor bills? How much could be saved in unnecessary dental bills, if junk foods were eliminated?
- *Education:* Are those lessons really necessary?
- *Life insurance:* Can whole-life be switched to term insurance?
- *Gifts:* What creative family projects can be started to give meaningful one-of-a-kind gifts?
- *Transportation:* How much debt and monthly expense could be saved through the sale of our best car? By reducing driving by 20%?

Table 8: Sample Budget
Husband: Age 34 Wife: Age 34 Child: Age 10 Child: Age 8
Our Financial Goals

	Monthly	Annually	Percent of Income
1. Tithes and offerings	125	1,500	10%
2. Federal income tax	101	1,212	8%
3. State income tax	12	144	1%
4. Social Security tax	76	912	6%
5. Other taxes (such as city)			
6. Shelter *	333	3,996	27%
7. Food	200	2,400	16%
8. Clothing	60	720	5%
9. Health	50	600	4%
10. Education	15	180	1%
11. Life insurance	15	180	1%
12. Gifts	20	240	2%
13. Transportation **	166	1,992	13%
(10,000 mi. @ $.20 mi.)			
14. Personal allowances	30	360	2%
15. Vacations			
16. Savings	47	564	4%
17. Household purchases			
18. Debt reduction			
19.			
20.			
21.			
Totals	$1,250	$15,000	100%

* *Assumptions:*

Mortgage payment on house	$180.00	per month, on a
Real estate tax	400.00	mortgage of $18,000;
Personal property tax	100.00	annual interest is
Sales and gas tax	258.00	$1,800

** *Car:*

Gas (20 mpg at $1.00 per gallon)	500.00
Repairs ($.04 per mile)	400.00
Insurance	300.00
Taxes	80.00
For car replacement	712.00

- *Personal allowance:* How much would we save if each of us had a firm limit on cash spent each week for candy, pop, coffee, magazines, and stuff?
- *Vacations:* Should our family vacation this year be a time of earning, instead of giving in to our yearnings?
- *Household purchases:* Have we tried the garage sales for our absolute needs? (After praying, of course!)
- *Debt reduction:* Just picture no more payments! *Ever!* Now SQUEEZE all you can for those debt payments. How much could you add to your debt payments if you worked in your neighborhood, for church members, on Saturdays?

Put the pencil to the answers to those questions and the eraser to your first figures. Keep figuring and erasing until the budget balances (income equals expenses) and you have the peace of God in your heart about your spending plan.

To stimulate your own thinking, I've included a sample budget for a family of four trying to balance a debt-free budget on a $15,000 annual gross income. Use it as a starting point for working out your own spending plan.

3. Start keeping records. The purpose of keeping records is to see how you're doing compared to your plan.

One way to maintain a good family budget would be to open up thirteen different checking accounts at the bank. Each bank account would represent a different spending category. Out of each paycheck you would deposit up to your spending plan in each account. For example, if you planned to spend $333 a month in shelter, you'd deposit $333 during the month in your shelter checking account. As you wrote checks for your rent or house payment, utilities, repairs, and household supplies, you'd list the checks on your check register and subtract the amounts from your balance in the bank. At the end of the month you'd know these two things: how much you spent according to your plan and where you spent the money.

A shelter-checking-account check register would look like this:

		March Deposit			3/1	333	00	333	00
1	3/4	First Mortgage Co. - Hse Pmt	180	00				153	00
2	3/8	United Telephone - Mo. Bill	8	75				144	25
3	3/12	Blue Flame Gas Co. - Mo. Bill	17	25				127	00
4	3/18	Clean Elec. Co. - Mo. Bill	22	80				104	20
5	3/26	Bud's Electric - Oven Repair	32	20				72	00
6	3/28	Quick Trash - 3 mo's Mo. Pay	5	50				66	50
7	3/30	Fuller Brush - Household Supplies	18	40				48	10
8	3/30	Dr. Thomas - Vet Dog Care	8	10				40	00
9	3/31	Envelope	15	00				25	00

In this example, your first eight checks to specific companies and individuals have used all but $40 of your plan.

The last check was for cash to keep in a shelter envelope. You'd write the check to your bank and get fifteen one-dollar bills to keep in a stationery envelope marked *shelter*.

You'd use this money to replace cash you spent for items connected with shelter. Such purchases might be for a can of paint, some weed killer, a light bulb, flashlight batteries, floor wax, or a broom. You need not keep track of money removed from the shelter envelope, since you've already listed it as a shelter expense when you put it into the envelope.

Don't panic! I'm not really telling you to open thirteen checking accounts. I've used this method to illustrate what you are doing when you keep a budget. Instead of the thirteen checking accounts, you can keep one checking account. Your budget book will have thirteen spending accounts in which you show deposits for the amounts you intend to spend in each area. (You list the checks that are to be charged to each spending account.) By subtracting each check listed from the amount you planned to spend, you can see at all times how you are doing compared to your plan.

And that's what budgeting is all about. That's planned spending. That's telling your money where you want it to go, instead of wondering where it went.

You may be able to set up and keep a budget from what you've read here. If so, any notebook or record book with columns such as these will suffice: Vernon Royal makes record books that are called *Cash, Journal* and *S. E. Journal.* Most office supply stores carry these or similar books.

You might like to buy a book that will have the forms all laid out for you, along with biblical encouragements and specific instructions. Your Christian bookstore should have or can order either of these two planning guides: *Financial Planning Guide for Your Money Matters* by Malcolm Mac-Gregor (Bethany Fellowship, Inc., Minneapolis, MN, 1978). *God's Answers to Financial Problems* by Rick Yohn (Harvest House Publishers, Irvine, CA, 1978). Another excellent workbook is *Family Financial Planning Workbook* by Larry Burkett and Horace Holley (Christian Financial Concepts, Tucker, GA, 1977). (You may order direct from the publisher: 290A Norcross–Tucker Road, Norcross, GA 30071).

If you have been motivated to start a budget, don't put it off. Let me encourage you with a fun portion of Scripture: "Then the Lord said to Moses, 'Quit praying and get the people moving! Forward, march!' " (Exodus 14:15 LB).

Get started now! The debts you pay will be your own. The tithe you give will be a blessing. The budget you balance will bring peace to your heart and joy to your life.

"The desire accomplished is sweet to the soul . . ." (Proverbs 13:19 KJV).

Illustration by
Mrs. Lynn Nolte

Marjean's 2¢: "The Honeymoon Is Over!"

One day, after a seminar in California, a woman handed me a card on which she had written, "The honeymoon is over, as well as I can judge it; he's taken her off the pedestal and put her on a budget."

Many women have that feeling. I can remember feeling very "put upon," when George asked me to post to the budget book. Complaining thoughts raced through my mind. "What do I know about *his* budget?" "I'll make mistakes!" "I don't have time to do that." "That's *his* thing!"

Unwillingly, I said I'd do it to "help him out, this time." I did make mistakes. Math and I were never on good terms. I really had a hang-up in that area. I felt guilty when he patiently taught me how to do it and never jumped me when he found mistakes, as I thought he would do. With his tender but firm encouragement, I gained more confidence. Joyce Landorf calls that being "tough yet tender"—tough enough to stick to his guns, but tender in his teaching.

Before I knew it, I was given more responsibility in keeping our finances in order.

Perhaps you can identify with me in the preceding description. If so, you and I can easily let our husbands assume the ultimate responsibility of the finances of the home and let them delegate duties to us that support them. Each of our jobs is equally important. We simply assume different roles.

Some of you wives may realize that you have had

more training in this area, so you can handle it more easily than your husbands. Remember that it took you a long time to learn finances, so your husband needs time and understanding from you. It is God's plan for the man to be the head of the home, and finance is one important area for him to carry out God's plan (*see* 1 Corinthians 11:3). As his helpmeet, you can help him assume his God-given role. Remember that he will become stronger as you lean on him.

With the blurring of roles in today's society, I am constantly hearing women say that their husbands never pay any attention to the finances, but leave it all to them. On questioning each woman closely, I discover that, early in her marriage, she made her husband feel he was incompetent; or she refused to pay any attention to his attempt at regulating their spending, so he gave up. According to Dr. Harold M. Voth, "In 70% of the families, men do not attend to the family finances." Each partner goes his or her own way, and the couple usually follows the way of debt, arguing, and misery.

We've had struggles in our marriage. I can remember a New Year's Eve when George chose to go over our budget. The evening was ruined as I dissolved in tears when we discovered *I* had gone over in the food category. I hadn't learned how to keep close watch on the budget book and let it help me stay within our plan.

Furthermore, I was defensive and felt George was criticizing me. All the budget book was, in the beginning, was a record of what we spent rather than an indicator of how we were doing on our spending plan. Now, I realize George and I need to use the budget book to guide us. As we have learned to communicate better in this area, each of our responsibilities has been determined.

My responsibilities have developed into:

• paying the bills on time (I have a special box where the bills are placed when they arrive, until bill-paying time).

• keeping an accurate check stub and a running balance in the checkbook. (I am careful to write the exact amount of the check on the stub, rather than rounding up or down. Don't laugh—some do!)

• filing the receipts in an organized way. An expanding alphabetized file box is very handy.

• reconciling the bank statement soon after it arrives, to make sure the checkbook and bank agree.

• posting the checks to the categories in the budget book.

• being willing to ask George for help in checking the budget book regularly, so he can keep abreast of the condition of each category. We are in this together, so we need to work together.

• being committed to the plan. This last responsibility is extremely important, for I believe it is workable and helpful. If I am faithful in carrying it out, it *will* work. In our case, our responsibilities are divided, in that I keep track of the outgo, and George keeps track of the income and of me. And we've done this by mutual agreement.

In keeping this kind of budget for our spending for twenty-five years, I have reaped great benefits.

Record keeping has restrained spending. For example, I resisted that beautiful leather purse, because it was not in the budget. By cleaning and polishing the old one, I found that it would do just as well.

The budget has helped me become my husband's helpmeet in an important area. As most couples will admit, to be able to talk openly in the area of family finances is helpful in building a good foundation for communication.

Our children have not only witnessed God's principles and the techniques in action, but they have also seen mom and dad work together in the vital area of marriage. I hope this example will carry over into their homes.

I also recognize that this careful training has helped prepare me for widowhood. I must face the fact that statistics show that the average wife lives seven years longer than her husband. I'm thankful I won't face those years afraid that I don't know how to handle money.

By being good stewards of what God has entrusted to us, we have been able to give more to our Lord and to His work. I've had to learn to be a "cheerful giver." It has taken time for me to understand that the following verse does work practically: "And God is able to provide you with every blessing in abundance, so that you may always have enough of everything and may provide in abundance for every good work" (2 Corinthians 9:8 RSV). There's no question that our budget has been one of God's great blessings. He has given me the power to be obedient to His will. You, too, can experience God's blessings in this area. Are you willing to be obedient to Him? Examine your heart and see if you are allowing your husband to lead you. Are you like the wise woman of Proverbs 14:1 (LB) who ". . . builds her house . . ." (by keeping a budget) or like the foolish woman, who ". . . tears hers down by her own efforts" (by overspending and being impractical, unwilling to be taught, and discontented with the way your husband provides for you)?

Why not determine now, with God's help, to follow His will by not hindering your husband but "helping him all the days of your life" (*see* Proverbs 31:12) and keeping on a budget?

Answers to Budgeting Questions

1. How can I avoid adding to my Sears Easy Payment plan? It is time to buy school clothes, and there is no cash available. Jesus gave us a simple formula: "Ask, and it will be given you . . ." (Matthew 7:7 RSV). So pray about the school clothes. Tell the Lord exactly what your children *need*. Purpose to trust God, not a loan. Make a list of the *essentials*. Try the thrift stores, garage sales, or other sources.

2. How do you find the balance between budgeting and making wise deals? Budgeting is planned spending which leads to wise deals. A budget will allow you to plan to buy fall school clothes at the end of winter, when they are on sale—not at the beginning of school, when they are in great demand.

3. About what percentage of your monthly income should you budget for clothing? The experts say not over 10% of your spendable income should be for clothes. We find that 10% of our income for clothes would be exorbitant.

4. *How do you know how much to allow for income tax, when each year your earnings increase and you owe more than your estimated taxes?* Figure what percent of your total income last year's state and federal taxes were. Whenever your current month's income exceeds last year's income, set aside in a special savings account that same percent of the additional income. Then you'll probably be prepared at tax time.

5. *How can a budget be worked out for a person whose income is irregular in amount and never catches up with present obligations? Where is the handle?* Every successful budget has this handle: The income is greater than the expenditures. If income *never* catches up with present obligations, the spending must be cut.

6. *Our income is flexible, as my husband is self-employed (he's a doctor). It seems impossible to have a budget and keep it on target. Any suggestions?* Plan your spending on a level monthly budget. Withdraw from his practice, each month, the amount you plan to spend. Put the rest in savings. If he earns less in a month than you plan to spend, withdraw the difference from your savings.

7. *How long should you keep your records?* With a single budget book for each of our twenty-five years of marriage, I see no reason to destroy any of them. You may want to write a book someday about your experiences.

8. *How much should a family of five (three small children) allow for groceries?* Government figures show that food costs from 20% down to 12% of gross income, with the higher percentages starting with the lower incomes and decreasing to the higher incomes. The sample budget in this chapter has a 16% food category for the $15,000 income.

> ### *Marjean's Response*
> I want to comment about the question of whether we practice what we teach.
>
> A few years ago George suggested that, perhaps, since we had been keeping a budget for several years and our finances seemed in good shape, we could do away with the labor of keeping a budget.
>
> I protested immediately. Having worked at this plan for so many years, I was beginning to learn how to let it work for me.
>
> In the clothes category, I know exactly how much money I have to spend or need to save up in order to buy an article of clothing. In the food category, I plan the amount of the check I write each week, in order to stay within the allotted amount.
>
> I just don't know how I could operate without a budget! I certainly wouldn't even want to try.

9. Do you practice what you tell us, to the last detail? What is the reaction of your family to your budget? Do you stand fast and carry this out now? Questions are often asked about whether we live what we write and speak about. We try to. Marjean and I have enjoyed the profit from twenty-five years of budgeting. It has enabled us to reach our recent goal of giving the Lord more than we spend for living expenses. That's why we still stand fast to a budget now.

10. How do you set up a budget for a person who has never had any practice in keeping records? Start simply. Try to plan one spending category, such as food. Keep track of all cash spent and checks written for all food purchases. Then compare food spending to the plan. Once it has been done in one area, it can be done in all others.

11. How do you make a decision on spending money for maintenance of someone else's well-meaning offer of a gift to you? Before receiving a gift, count the cost. I once turned down the gift of a country-club membership, because, among other reasons, I did not want to spend money on the monthly dues.

12. What is depreciation? Is it any use to family budget planning? How? Depreciation is the difference between what you pay for an item and what it can be sold for at any given time. The best use in the family budget is to plan to set aside enough money to be able to replace items that will wear out, such as the car, washer, dryer, air conditioner, furnace, and a host of other items.

13. How do you keep financially on top of bills if your husband's job is seasonal or unstable at times? His job pays well when he works, but usually we can almost count on at least a month and one-half off, each year. Total your annual income. Divide that figure by the ten months he works, to see how to plan your monthly spending. During the months he works, set aside, in a savings account, all his income over the monthly spending plan. During the "off" months you should have enough to withdraw for your spending needs.

14. How can I keep a balanced budget? A "balanced budget" means that income at least equals spending. Most people balance their budgets by controlling their spending.

15. Is it necessary to write down everything I spend, to be on a budget? Not necessarily. Example: Write a check for $25 for food. Keep the money in a separate coin purse, and always use it only for food. You write down only the $25 check in your budget book. When your coin purse is empty, you know that the $25 has gone for food.

There's no need to keep track of where you spent it. But be honest.

16. *How can I know where my money is going, if the budget doesn't balance?* Only by keeping records of your spending can you know where your money is going. This is true whether you balance your budget or not.

17. *Do you have any information regarding the establishment of a realistic budget that could be used in a family? Oftentimes people either overestimate or underestimate their financial capabilities and use of their income.* A budget is a series of financial goals for a particular family. Each family will set its own goals, based on its own priorities. For example, our family has always placed our home higher on the spending category than our car. Consequently, our home has been more adequate, while our cars have all been bought used.

We've valued savings for education more highly than clothes or furniture. Consequently, we've had funds set aside for college for our daughters, but we've done without many clothing wants and bought lots of used furniture, carpets, and other household items.

Each family must make its own choices, and you must face the facts of your own situation.

18. *Why are records of past payments important in knowing where your money went?* Without records, you'll deceive yourself on where your money really goes. When I give people the assignment to record all their spending for a week, the are always amazed at how much money they spent on meaningless items.

With records, you'll spot errors more easily. One month, at my business, one of my incoming toll-free telephone bills more than doubled. By producing records for my previous six months of bills, I showed the phone company that my current bill was unreasonable. Sure enough, their computer had gone awry.

Records settle disputes, save time, and help in future planning.

19. *How can you best plan a budget, without really knowing what the cost of living and other expenditures will be?* With living costs rising regularly, budgeting is a necessity. Each year's spending plan includes increases in certain spending areas. For example, within the same living quarters, you would need to plan on spending a larger amount than you spent last year for utilities.

7 Seeing the Working-Mother Squeeze

Will you assume with me that one good reason most mothers work is for the money? Since, in the United States, 41% of mothers with children under age six work outside the home, the financial benefits must be tremendous.

But they aren't! Especially for the working wife and mother.

Figures show that women still earn less than men. The usually accepted figure is that for every dollar in the male's pay envelope, the female finds only sixty cents.

The Bottom Line for the Working Mother

What is the potential net income of a working wife and mother? We'll give two examples, both of which assume that the husband is making $12,000 a year, that there are two children involved, that the family tithes its gross income, and that the wife is not a professional in a high-income bracket.

	Example 1	Example 2	Fill in Yours
Wife's gross income per year	$6,084.00	$9,152.00	_____
Wife's gross income per week	117.00	176.00	_____
Wife's expenses:			
Tithe	11.70	17.60	_____
Federal income tax	21.03	33.82	_____
State income tax	5.50	9.73	_____
Social Security tax	7.17	10.79	_____
Transportation	8.00	8.00	_____
(10 trips of 4 miles @ $.20 a mile)			
Lunch and coffee breaks	9.00	9.00	_____
Restaurants and carry-outs	12.00	15.00	_____
Extra clothes	10.00	12.00	_____
Beauty shop	9.00	9.00	_____
Other bought-it-with-my-money expenses	6.00	12.00	_____
Babysitting	30.00	30.00	_____
(1 child preschool)			
Totals	$129.40	$166.94	_____
Net addition to family income:	−$12.40	$9.06	_____

At the $12,000 level the family's federal tax for 1978 would be approximately $827. Kansas state tax would total $154.

For the wife, the additional $6,084 of her income, after tithe, would leave $5,476 taxable. This income adds $1,094 federal tax and $286 state tax, plus $373 for Social Security—a grand total of $1,753, or a whopping 28.8% of all she earns.

For the higher-paid wife, earning 50% more than minimum wage, the results are even more astounding. The additional $9,152 income adds up to $8,237 taxable. Federal taxes will claim $1,759, state taxes $506, and Social Security $561—the horrendous total of $2,826—30.9% of all she earns.

Those Pesky Extra Expenses

One of my friends is a business executive. His wife works part time for the enjoyment of it and for some extra money. When he figured his taxes this year, he noted that 58% of all she earned went out for federal, state, and Social Security taxes. When I asked him if she spent only 42% of what she made, he just laughed. From observation, we both knew the answer to my question.

Assuming a commitment to pay God and Caesar, the tax and tithe amounts are not open to debate. Let's examine the other expense categories:

Transportation The assumption is that the working mother will drive forty more miles each week going to and from sitters and to and from work than if she were not working. Assuming she's driving an older car that is paid for, she's spending $.20 a mile (for gas, oil, repairs, and some set aside to replace the car she's driving), for an additional weekly spending of $8.

Her weekly driving totals 172 more miles a month than if she were not working. Your records may show that the working mother drives less when she is working, because she doesn't have all day to shop, take the children on visits, and other ways of driving around. My own observation is that the working mothers often use their cars to shop on the lunch hours, and do more driving in the evenings and on Saturdays, in an attempt to take the children out.

Marjean never worked outside the home. Careful records revealed that her total driving during the children's preteen years never exceeded 4,000 miles a year (77 miles weekly). Expert planning enabled her to do all her shopping, church work, doctor visits, children's parties, lessons, and school functions within the 4,000 miles a year. With both teenagers driving, the total jumped to 9,700 miles during those high-school years.

Keep mileage records. You'll soon know whether your working adds to your miles driven or not.

Lunches and coffee breaks   Most working mothers have little time for lunch preparation from refrigerator leftovers. Coffee, soft drinks, and snacks during the "sacred" coffee breaks easily add $.20 to $.40 a day to expenses. The sky's the limit on purchased lunches, but counting tips and taxes, you could reasonably average $1.50 for a bowl of soup or a small salad and iced tea. The $1.50 daily lunch, plus an average of $.30 for snacks, totals $9 weekly.

You may spend more or less. Again, some record keeping will be the key to your real expenses.

Restaurants and carry-outs   Show me a working mother who doesn't take her family out to eat more than the nonworking mother, and I'll show you a rare woman.

Fast-food industry figures show that approximately 30% of all food dollars are spent eating meals away from home. The proof is in the line of Wendy's, McDonald's, Denny's, Burger Chef, Pizza Hut, and other places that occupy prominent locations in almost any American town with a population over 15,000. They are in business because we are eating out more than ever before.

Before you say that your own family certainly doesn't spend 30% of your food dollars eating out, compare your spending with the chart below.

Monthly food budget	$200.00	$250.00	$300.00	$350.00
Weekly food budget	46.51	58.13	69.76	81.39
Thirty percent of weekly budget	13.95	17.44	20.93	24.41

The more the mother makes, the more likely she is to spend for the "treats" out. Let's see what the $12 and $15 estimated per week would buy for our family of four.

McDonald's	1 Big Mac	$ .95	
	1 Cheeseburger	.50	
	2 Hamburgers	.90	
	2 Fries	.80	
	4 Medium Cokes	1.80	
	2 Fried pies	.70	$5.65
		Tax	.17
		Total	$5.82
Long John Silver's	2 Fish plates	4.18	
	2 Child's specials	1.98	
	4 Medium drinks	1.60	$7.76
		Tax	.23
		Total	$7.99
Baskin Robbins	4 Double-dip cones	$2.92	

With two such elegant meals out and one ice-cream treat, you've spent $16.73 for the week. And if you go to a cafeteria for a Sunday lunch, instead, the family of four could barely escape for $12, as hungry as you all are after a quick Sunday breakfast, Sunday school, and church. With this combination, your family has only eaten twelve meals away from home, out of eighty-four meals in a week for your family. Adding lunches for the working mother and father and the kids at school or at the sitter's, you may easily be eating thirty-two of those eighty-four meals a week away from home.

Using the eat-at-home principle, you could get Colonel

Sanders' fried-chicken dinner for four with fries and spend a modest $8.70, or a large Pizza Hut pizza for $7.80.

Be honest. Because you work, do you and your family eat more meals out? Your figures may be lower or higher than the ones estimated.

Extra clothes   Most working mothers find that their wardrobes need to be larger for work than if they are full-time homemakers. The pressure from co-workers who show up each season in new styles takes its toll. The wear and tear on clothing worn all day, at regular intervals, is a factor. The need for a nicer coat, to replace the one you've made do—which looks more shabby, since you wear it daily in all kinds of weather—will provoke you to buy a new coat.

An extra $10 a week will allow one item weekly to be dry-cleaned and about $8 for extra purchases. Depending on the quality of dresses, coats, blouses, pantsuits, sweaters, slacks, coats, raincoats, shoes, lingerie, and gloves you buy, your expenses may be more or less than our example.

My own experience is that working mothers feel that, out of the $6,000 to $9,000 they earn, they're justified in dressing a "little nicer." And the more they earn, the more they spend.

Beauty shop   A working mother has precious little time to care for herself or to sit peacefully in a quiet place. Most feel that the beauty-shop routine helps their spirits and their looks. As I head to town shortly after 6:00 a.m., I'm always surprised to see open beauty shops. They open early to serve working women.

The cost? Minimum here in Wichita these days seems to be $9 for a shampoo and set. You'd need to add $30 to $45 more for a periodic permanent, cutting, or tinting, or an occasional manicure. And don't forget to count the stuff you buy that sits in sight while your hair is drying. Such displays are not accidents, for people often buy what is close at hand.

You may or may not have this expense.

Bought-it-with-my-money expenses You're earning six to nine thousand a year, or even more. Why not a little splurge now and then for the family!

- Extra clothes for the children
- More expensive Christmas gifts
- A skiing vacation at spring break
- Something really nice that your husband's always wanted, but could never afford
- A special meal out with your husband, at a really nice restaurant

My experience in this area is that $9 to $12 a week for such items would prove to be conservative in the course of a full year.

Babysitting The going rate in Wichita, Kansas, now is $30 to $40 per child, per week. For younger school-age children, who need care in the early morning and after school, the weekly cost is $20 to $30. What are your child-care costs?

Is It Worth It?

Total all your extra expenses that are connected with your work. Subtract those expenses from your earnings, and you have what is called "the bottom line": your profit from your work, the amount you keep as a result of all the hours you are away from children and home in order to work.

What is your net? Now divide it by the fifty hours you are away from home, driving to and from work, working, and lunch times, and you see your hourly net income. Take a good long hard look at it!

Is your working worth the cost? Your cost is the taxes and expenses. Your cost is having someone else spend those fleeting hours with your children. Your cost is being a part-time helper to your husband. Your cost is busy, busy, busy. What do you think?

Questions

1. What about the doctors who recommend a wife work, for her own therapy, even if she makes nothing in the long run? Each couple must decide the work question, before the Lord. Most women work to make money so the family can spend more.

Work *is* good medicine. Depression usually sets in when anyone does not accept the responsibilities God has given. For the wife and mother, these responsibilities include meeting the husband's needs, housekeeping, cooking, household management, and child care.

The mother who needs the exhilaration of a paycheck to meet her emotional needs will possibly never be content with what that paycheck will do for her and her family. The weekly wages certainly will never do for her husband and her children what *she* could do with her creative energies applied in the home.

2. I have a part-time job and believe I do make money at it. What if a woman's creative abilities are in the area of outside work, rather than cooking, sewing, and other such things? Part-time work is often a solution to a family's needs. One man came to me after he had bought a house, knowing his wife needed to go to work to help meet the additional expenses of the larger house. I asked him how much additional income they needed. He didn't know. We calculated it. Would you believe that their need was for less than a half-time job would pay? Yet, she had been planning to leave home for the whole day, entrust their six-year-old to a sitter, and find the highest-paying job she could get.

We prayed for a specific part-time job between the hours

of 9:00 A.M. and 3:00 P.M., within one mile of their home, that would pay enough, after tithe and taxes, to meet their needs.

God answered! She got the job, was home till her son left for school, and back when he returned. The neighborhood job allowed her to spend very little time driving to and from work. She liked the variety, but still had time to concentrate on the home and her husband.

3. How do you feel about a mother's going to work to help pay for a child's college education? I feel that you should get the facts about the bottom line before you leave home to work for that purpose.

Consider the fact of your state's guidelines of family income for tuition grants. Consider the federal government's income limits for eligibility for certain government grants to students. There are many cases in which the mother's income has increased the family income to such a level that the student became ineligible for grants that would have been available based only on the father's income.

Consider also the fact that a dependent student can earn tax-free (except for Social Security) income of $3,400 during any year that the parents provide over one-half of the student's living expenses.

Check with the school's financial aid director and with an accountant before you decide to take a job just to meet college expenses.

8 *Avoiding the Newlywed Squeeze*

Would you like some fatherly advice from an experienced bill collector? Would you like some positive, practical steps you can take to insure that your marriage will not suffer from financial problems? Set a goal *now* to be *financially free.*

My friend Jim Underwood, president of the National Institute of Christian Financial Planning, called from Florida while I was writing this book. He is a frequent teacher of seminars designed to assist participants in the accomplishment of their God-given goals. His group has done financial counseling with more than 5,000 couples. What do you think they found to be the number-one problem of most couples? It was: *Failure to identify goals.* A couple without financial goals will very quickly drift into debt, buying things they want, with money they don't have.

Fit to Be Tied, or Just Knotted

The average young couple I counsel has been married two or three years. Both have jobs, regular earnings, no

112

financial goals, no budget, big debts, and plenty of arguments about money. Their debts usually total between $8,000 and $10,000.

Not a single couple has ever told me, "Well, we did it. By our deliberate overspending, we've reached our three-year goal of owing $10,000. Our frequent arguments over money and the financial pressures we feel are just what we planned. The thrill we feel as we look forward to paying off these debts is the highlight of our marriage." That's not what they say. They do ask, "How did it happen? Why didn't somebody tell us about debt?"

Do you know what a $10,000 debt means? Not just that they owe the credit-card companies a total of $10,000. But that their monthly interest due totals $150. Did you see that clearly? One hundred and fifty dollars a month due in interest! And the monthly payment to pay off the $10,000 debt in four years at the 18% interest rate will total $293.75. Think of it: for the next four years, forty-eight months, a regular payment on debt every month of $293.75. A total of $14,100.

When I tell the couple what it will take to pay off those debts, they are stunned. "How will we do it? We haven't been able to make it *without* making all these debt payments? How will we do it *with* them?"

"Painfully!" is my answer.

Let me show you how painful such payments will be. Sit down now with your fiancé or your new spouse. Develop a spending plan by going over Our Financial Goals in chapter six. When you are through, add in debt payments of $293.75. Does your budget balance now? I've never seen one that does.

How much better to find out that you can't afford debt payments *now*, rather than after you're committed to forty-eight months of them.

What does it mean to be *financially free*? I asked that question of Jim Underwood, who gave me this answer:

Being financially free means living without *any* of these symptoms of personal financial problems:

1. You are preoccupied with thoughts about money, at the expense of thoughts about God.
2. You don't give what you feel God wants you to give.
3. You are not at peace to live on what God has provided.
4. You argue within your family about money matters.
5. You can't or don't pay credit cards in full each month.
6. You need or have considered a consolidation loan.
7. You receive notices of past-due accounts.
8. You charge items because you can't pay cash.
9. You use spending as emotional therapy.
10. You spend impulsively.
11. You invade savings to meet current expenses.
12. Your net worth does not increase annually.
13. You "just can't save."
14. You are underinsured.
15. You wish you had a plan for spending and saving and are frustrated because you don't.

If you want to avoid any and all of these fifteen symptoms, you'll set your goal to be financially free. But it will take two *basic* decisions. By facing these two decisions now, you are virtually assured of getting a super-fast start on your goal of being financially free.

> *No debt*   Decide at the outset that you will not spend what you do not have. "No money—no spendee."
> *Trust God instead of trusting a loan*   Turn to God instead of to the finance company. You'll find God more economical and much more merciful.

Marjean and I made this decision twenty-five years ago, when we were first married. We have never borrowed any money for anything other than the two houses we've bought.

Do you think we have ever for one minute regretted that decision? We have not. And we've never been sorry that we've had no debt payments to include in our annual budget.

And we have been willing to have had for other purposes the $18,000 most folks have spent for interest on their debts during their twenty-five years of marriage.

Marjean's 2¢: Conversation in the Ladies' Room

One evening, after dining out, I visited the ladies' room. While I was out of sight, two young women walked in. Their voices and conversation told me they were young. One, obviously not married, remarked to the other, "I always thought marriage was so great, but all I've heard is what problems there are."

The Mrs. replied, "June, let me tell you. It isn't all I thought it would be. It's not easy! This business of finances is a real struggle. Bob and I have been fighting more and more, and it's all over money. There never seems to be enough. Marriage is great, and I'd do it again in a minute, but I'd do things differently."

Do you suppose those things she'd do differently would be not to charge, to live on her husband's, and perhaps her, salaries, and to be content to buy only what they could afford?

I have loving memories of spreading the tablecloth on the floor for an "indoor picnic" when my new husband invited more guests for dinner than our card table and chairs would hold. I didn't think about going out and charging a bigger table and more chairs or denying George the privilege of sharing his new bride's cooking.

When our oldest daughter, Jenny, and her husband, Greg, were married, they lived in a basement apartment furnished with an old couch the school provided, a borrowed bed, a bean-bag chair, a small table, and two chairs. When they finished school and found jobs, their incomes were small. So they didn't have much when they moved out of the school housing into another basement apartment. It was amazing for us to see how frugally they lived and saved their money. We were excited when their better jobs earned them enough money so they could move into a real upstairs apartment. They are still saving to buy their furniture. I'm sure they'll appreciate it when they get it. And fights over money pressures have not been among their problems.

We continued to wait for what we could afford. In the house George and I built in 1957, we didn't have enough furniture for both the family room and living room, so we left the living room bare: no furniture and no carpet, drapes, or light fixtures.

The other day, a friend who sold us our air conditioner (which we waited to put in the house till the next summer, when we had the cash) remarked, "Well, one thing about you two: You have lived what you've talked. I remember over twenty years ago, when I came out to your house to figure your air-conditioner needs, and you didn't have a stick of furniture in your living room. George said he'd rather be cool than have furniture."

People watch our lives. Do they measure up? Do they help or hinder our testimony?

Keep Records

Talk over and decide now how you plan to spend your income. Set up a written budget, using the ideas presented in chapter six.

Remember that your budget is your tool to help you say *no* to the lesser so that you might gain the greater.

Decide that from this day forward you will include in your monthly spending plan each of these goals:

- Giving
- Saving
- Spending

Giving. You and I, who are God's people, are to be funnels for God's flow of resources. The Bible says, "Give, and it will be given to you . . . " (Luke 6:38 RSV). When the spout is blocked at the bottom, because of our stinginess, God can put nothing else in at the top.

Young couples often feel that they just don't have enough to give now. With their incomes low and their desires for furniture and stuff to fill the place where they live, there's just no money to give to the Lord. Such an analysis will prove that there's not enough to give and buy all those other things.

Giving to the Lord is not so much a matter of money as it is trusting God. When we give to the Lord first, we are really telling Him that we have the faith that He will replace it with more than enough to meet our needs. As our needs are met, we'll continue to be His channel for giving resources to others.

Are you trustworthy with what God has given you? Do you acknowledge that everything you have has come because God has made it possible?

A first-off-the-top-of-your-income tithe is the best way I know to prove to yourself and to demonstrate to God that you trust Him. One of my friends says that God is the only business manager in the world who can make 90% go farther than 100%.

Start your marriage as tithers. Know the joy and blessing of giving to others as you start your life learning to give to each other in marriage. The outflow of money from your new marriage will add to your relationship a certain rare quality that will be meaningful to you and attractive to others.

Saving. The excuses for not saving are the same as the reasons for not giving. With income low and desires high, right now is not the time to save.

Where giving is an act of faith, saving must be a habit of paydays. Paying yourself second (tithe is first) will insure that you regularly add to a small savings that will continually grow. Such savings will be your "never-to-spend" money. This money will be working for you each day of your life. If your never-to-spend savings totals $25 every month for the next forty years, and if that savings earns 5% per year, you'll have $38,411 in forty years. At that time you can leave it in at 5% interest and withdraw $160 a month, without touching the $38,411. Or you can withdraw $406 each month, for ten years, before your funds are exhausted.

The following item on saving appeared in the November 1978 *Cheer:*

> Andrew Carnegie once said: "The first thing that a man should learn to do is to save his money . . . . Thrift not only develops the fortune, but it develops also the man's character." Savings are your stored-up labor. You can exchange this stored-up labor for things you desire. The man who spends as he goes seldom goes far. A bank account raises a man's self-respect, enhances his manliness, increases his self-confidence, strengthens his peace of mind, and thereby makes him a better employee, a better citizen, a better father.
>
> B.C. FORBES

I've never seen a couple who ever regretted their decision to save money regularly. But I've seen hundreds of folks who wished they had started the savings habit before it was too late.

You will also need some savings to spend. Careful planning will have you save regularly, in advance, for purchases in the future. Such items as cars, furniture, major appliances, and college educations are items for which you can save.

Saving for purchases can save you large amounts of money. Look at this example of saving money to buy a used car. In checking your present car and its mileage, you decide that you will make it do for three more years. To prepare for that time, thirty-six months from now, when you will plan to replace your present car with a used one, you begin saving $90 a month. At an interest rate of 5%, you'll have $3,500 to pay for your used car. Your savings totaled $90 a month for thirty-six months, or a total of $3,240.

However, most people do not save for the purchase of a car. They tell me they just can't save for a car. So they justify financing the purchase of a car.

That's not right thinking. One of my definitions for debt is: "Savings in reverse, plus interest."

The very next month after people buy a car with money they don't have, they begin saving the money from their previous spending to pay the car payment. Let's see how much they need to save each month to pay off a $3,500 car in thirty-six months, with the interest cost to the consumer of 14%. The monthly payment to pay off the car in three years will be $120.49. The minute the car payment starts, the $120.49 has to be squeezed from their monthly budget. In thirty-six months, the total paid for that car would be $4,337.64.

What did the car cost the $90-a-month saver? $3,240.00! The difference is a staggering $1,097.64. The borrower paid 33.9% more for the car than the saver.

Can you imagine how much money Marjean and I have saved in twenty-five years by saving in advance for every purchase? Our savings came from several resources:

1. Interest earned while we saved to buy the item.
2. Interest not paid because of debt.
3. Bargains we took advantage of because we had the cash.
4. The natural restraint we exercised in most purchases, because we didn't plan to spend more for the item than we had saved for it.

Decide now to *save* for everything you ever buy. You'll save in more ways than one. You'll save arguments, frustration, stresses and strains, as well as interest.

Someone usually throws the old tax argument at me when I mention savings instead of debt. Since interest paid may be used as a tax deduction in using the long-form tax return, they mention the tax-saving feature of borrowing money. And, they smugly tell me, I didn't count the fact that taxes have to be paid on interest earned.

Marjean and I have delighted in taking our tax deductions for money given to the Lord's work. Generous givers have no trouble establishing tax deductions.

Spending. Your budget will be a boon to your spending. Just having a plan and then keeping records will bring huge rewards to you, financially. Here are some practical money-saving tips to help you during those first years of marriage.

Limit your eating out. Don't let anybody tell you it's cheaper than eating at home. Restaurant-industry figures show that food costs account for only 30% of total expenses. In your own apartment, you don't pay extra for the rent, advertising, insurance, taxes, cleanup, security, and labor. And you don't buy menus, extra dishes and glasses, or pay the cook and meal server. Those items, and many more, are included in the price of every meal you eat out.

Limit your T.V. watching. Dr. Ed Wheat, Christian physician and author, has developed a reputation as one of the country's leading authorities on physical intimacy in marriage. In his premarital counseling he gives a couple two pieces of advice for their first year of marriage. This advice is meant to enhance their sexual relationship: "Don't borrow money for any reason." "Don't own a television set."

You should discuss these decisions together and see how you think they could affect your relationship with each other.

Learn to create together. When you have a need, such as a table and chairs, be creative in locating other people's junk. (They sell their junk cheap.) Their junk can become your treasure.

Visualize what some repairs can mean to that old wood table. Picture how beautiful the top will be when you've filled in those holes and sanded the table down to its natural beauty. And think how pleased you'll be with this table when it's been stained or painted to blend in with your own home.

Marjean and I are still eating and serving meals to friends on a table we bought for under $30 several years ago. I'm still amazed that the antiquing job she did with less than $15 worth of supplies turned that junk table into an item of furniture that looks so nice in our home.

Limit your driving. How many people do you know who have a mileage budget for their cars? Driving costs money. The more miles you drive, the more money you spend. The more you drive, the sooner you will need tires and car repairs.

Find ways to cut your driving! Combine trips for shopping, visits, and entertainment. Enjoy days at home, when you never get in your car. Learn to use public transportation. Learn to walk and ride bikes. We have a shopping mall that is exactly a twenty-minute walk from our home. We enjoy walking there together to buy things we need. Seldom do we buy more than we need. Carrying it home on the twenty-minute walk can be a real burden.

Keep a predetermined amount of money with you. The total amount of money we had with us for the first twenty years of marriage was never more than $20. Our billfolds were each planned to be stocked with two $10 bills.

Whatever I spent of that $20 had to be replaced from our petty-cash envelopes at home. Knowing how much I originally had with me helped me determine what I'd bought with the amount that was spent but not recorded.

Include a small allowance for yourselves. A monthly amount of $5 to $20 should be yours to spend for whatever you want. I've used mine for haircuts, golf games, football tickets, a super sundae, magazines, and hundreds of other items. Marjean is delighted with these expenditures, because she knows that they are a part of the budget and that I'm not overspending our money when I blow my allowance.

Don't own a pet. Please don't report me to the Society for the Prevention of Cruelty to Animals. The fact that our little dachshund lived to be seventeen is partially due, I'm certain, to the daily walks she and I took during the last three years of her life.

Pets are expensive. Cat and dog food isn't cheap. When animals get hurt, most people take them to the vet. They weren't meant to exist in carpeted and draped homes and often cause considerable damage to home furnishings. Animal care, when you travel, is expensive.

One of our friends dog-sits every day for her daughter's and son-in-law's dog, while they work. She refers to the little dog as granddog.

The night Amy and her fiancé shared their wedding desires with Marjean and me, we had a real laugh. After we had expressed our agreement with their hopes, Amy said, "Hey, Mom and Dad, we have a wedding present for you: Chaussee! Mike doesn't like cats!" We'd been keeping Amy's kitty at home during her four years of college. Now, Chaussee looks like a permanent fixture.

I also greatly enjoy a beautiful keeshond named Elka. Every evening Elka comes to our back door, and I let her in. We talk and bark, romp, and have a great time. Then I give her one dog biscuit, and she leaves. When Marjean and I go on walks, Elka joins us; and we all have a ball.

Elka belongs to our next-door neighbor. I let him buy the food, pay the vet bills, and be awakened around 5:00 A.M. every day to let Elka out. What a neat way to enjoy a dog.

Pray together about financial decisions. When counseling a couple in money trouble, I frequently ask if they're praying together. Not just about money, but about everything.

Very few couples know the blessing that comes with prayer in marriage. But the Bible is full of promises about the special power that comes from the Lord when two pray together. Jesus Himself gave us one of those promises: "Again I say to you, if two of you agree on earth about anything they ask, it will be done for them by my Father in heaven. For where two or three are gathered in my name, there am I in the midst of them" (Matthew 18:19, 20 RSV). What more welcome place to have that special presence of God than in your young marriage relationship? As Marjean and I have prayed together, the Lord has blessed our praying, our relationship, and our home, in a very special way. Our prayer would be for your marriage to start financially free and to be fruitful in God's sight.

Questions

1. How can a husband suggest frugality without feeling stingy or seeming stingy to his wife? ". . . Reliable communication permits progress" (Proverbs 13:17 LB). A well-communicated plan for family spending should solve your problem. We all have to make choices in our spending, giving, and saving: We say *no* to this in order to say *yes* to that. If, after seeing the facts, your wife feels you are being stingy, together decide which spending category you will reduce in order to add to the category in which she feels pressure. It should not be a matter of stinginess, but of priorities.

2. What if the wife wants to tithe and the husband doesn't? What should she do? During a one-hour program in the Dallas area, where listeners were allowed to call in and ask questions, this was the most common question. The wife feels caught between the biblical principle of giving and the equally biblical principle of submission to her husband.

What should a wife do? Submit! "You wives must submit to your husbands' leadership in the same way you submit to the Lord. . . . So you wives must willingly obey your husbands in everything, just as the church obeys Christ" (Ephesians 5:22, 24 LB).

By submitting, the wife leaves the husband with the responsibility for giving. This is where it belongs. When she gives herself to her husband as a helpmeet, God may use her loving-servant attitude toward his needs and her giving spirit to develop in her husband a desire to become a giver. Such a desire seldom occurs when the wife gives in spite of her husband's desire that she not do so.

3. I have lived by the principles you teach and have stayed out of debt. Now I have remarried, and my husband doesn't believe or follow them. How can I deal with this situa-

tion? Again the answer is submission. God calls you to be submissive to your husband. God calls him to be responsible to Himself for the management of what money is entrusted to your family. Your prayers for your husband's obedience to God in financial principles will be a real help to your husband.

Marjean's 2¢: Husband and Wife

"Should I write the checks, or should my husband be responsible for that?" This is a frequent question women ask me, after one of George's finance seminars.

My answer is based on Ephesians 5:21–26. Paul declared, "Be subject to one another out of reverence for Christ" (verse 21 RSV). This instruction indicates a working together, a mutual understanding of each role in the marriage, as God has directed. The husband is the head, responsible for his wife's direction.

Therefore, in the case of money matters, if the husband directs his wife to pay the bills, keep the budget book, and take care of other financial details, yet still recognizes that he is ultimately responsible, then things are in order. The real key to the workability of this plan is the attitude of the husband and the wife. If they see themselves as one, each having different functions according to recognized gifts, then harmony will result. They are pulling together, rather than pulling apart.

Some women tell me that their husbands won't take the responsibility for the money. It is interesting to note that these same husbands have little or nothing to do with anything around the house or the children. I would venture to ask, "Have you let him?"

When our girls were little, I handled everything that had to do with them. I'd had all the child training; and George didn't know anything about it, I thought. I never gave him a chance to learn. Of course he felt awkward. He was an only child and hadn't even been around children. They looked to me for all decisions. I didn't realize that I was undermining George's authority and, consequently, their respect for him. Fortunately this changed as, through some Christian teaching, I discovered my mistake.

A friend of mine had been trained in the keeping of records and handling money. She wanted to live on a budget, but her husband showed no interest in it. So she kept records of all their expenditures. In her words, "I have three years of beautiful records, and I believe he is about ready to take charge." She hasn't pushed or nagged him about it. Instead, she has prayed and has done what she could to be ready when God got her husband's attention.

Another friend felt she could handle the record keeping much better than her husband, since he didn't like doing it. But she knew that she needed to wait on the Lord's timing. Her husband was convinced scripturally that they needed to keep records, so he decided to do it. But he hated every minute of it. He would grumble, get into bad moods, and finally quit, saying, "This won't work!" But, recognizing that this was God's way, and he "could do all things in Christ who strengthens him" (*see* Philippians 4:13), he would go back to it.

All the time, his wife was praying and trusting God. Finally he came to his wife and said, "I believe this will work, and I know you like to do this kind of thing, so I would like to ask you to keep the budget book." He didn't relinquish his responsibility; instead, he delegated this particular job to one who was better equipped to handle it. How much better for it to be handled this way, instead of the wife's just taking over and in this way belittling him.

9 S'more Unsqueezables

Do you remember those campfires where you ate s'mores? That combination of graham crackers, chocolate bars, and melted marshmallows was so tasty that you always wanted some more. Thus the name: s'mores.

Christian, what percent of your income are you giving to the Lord now: 1%, 5%, 10%, 20%, 50%? Whatever you're giving now, you probably would like to give s'more. More giving results in more blessings. These blessings include:

- *Gifts:* "give, and it will be given to you . . ." (Luke 6:38 RSV).
- *Love:* ". . . God loveth a cheerful giver" (2 Corinthians 9:7 KJV).
- *Riches:* ". . . you will always be rich enough to be generous" (2 Corinthians 9:11 NEB).
- *Joy:* "They begged us to take the money so they could share in the joy of helping the Christians in Jerusalem" (2 Corinthians 8:4 LB).

But inflation! With the cost of almost everything increasing steadily, most of us are struggling to keep our spending in line with our incomes.

And into my collection-agency office march dozens of Christians who have lost the spending battle and are mired deep in the debt trap. What amount do you need each month to pay your way out of the debt trap: $50, $100, $150, $200?

S'more Ways Out

With debts and inflation plaguing us, what practical, biblical steps are available to help us reduce our spending so we can dramatically increase our giving and/or our debt payments?

Did you know the Bible has principles to guide us in our spending? And each principle is a two-fold benefit: You have money saved, and you are God blessed.

The Bible says, "But he who looks into the perfect law, the law of liberty, and perseveres, being no hearer that forgets but a doer that acts, he shall be blessed in his doing" (James 1:25 RSV). If you want God's blessing on your spending, look at the biblical principles in this chapter and implement them into your own personal finances. And for each principle you obey, you may expect to cut your spending to the glory of God.

Avoid debt. The most frequently violated money command in Scripture in my experience is ". . . be content with your wages" (Luke 3:14 KJV). The sure sign of violation of this Scripture is overspending your pay.

The easiest way to allow your spending to get out of control is to succumb to the minimum-payment charge account and the good-almost-everywhere credit cards (*see* chapter 1).

The only thing easy about one "easy payment" is the ease of buying to accumulate large balances on your account. Most of you, along with hundreds of people I've counseled, can testify that repaying those runaway revolving accounts is tough stuff. From my vantage point, there are no entanglements more strangling than the mounting pressure of debts.

Counselees bring me glowing reports of less spending and balanced budgets, after that great family-credit-card-destruction ceremony. That's the time when you gather, as a family, to destroy all credit cards by cutting them into small pieces. Then you commit yourselves to one another to buy with cash only. All testify that cash spending is a real money-saving revelation.

With installment debt averaging $7,000 for each American family, an interest rate of 18% results in a monthly interest payment of $105. You can see that avoiding debt may save you approximately $105 a month. Isn't that a tremendous profit resulting from obedience to God's Word, "Owe no man any thing . . ."? (Romans 13:8 KJV).

Commit yourself today to ". . . make do with your pay" (Luke 3:14 NEB). If you don't have it, don't spend it. Do without! Postpone! Fix it up! Make do!

Plan your spending. Most people don't plan their spending. Jesus instructed us to count the cost: "For which one of you, when he wants to build a tower, does not first sit down and calculate the cost, to see if he has enough to complete it?" (Luke 14:28 NAS).

The record in my counseling is unbroken. It's my experience that if you are not operating on a budget, you are wasting between $50 and $175 a month. When you've established a plan for your spending, you'll frequently find yourself using those money-saving, almost magical five little words, *It's not in the budget!*

Nowhere is planned spending more important than in certain "budget busters." Any well-managed household can turn from success to failure on any one of these three:

- Vacations
- Christmas
- Back to school

A vacation without a budget is a family disaster. Heading cross-country, with no spending plan, often ends with surprise debts.

One enterprising family split its vacation funds in half. All the family knew was that they would travel as long and as far as the first half of the money lasted. With the other half, they would return home. They traveled much farther than they had expected and returned home having spent no more than they had planned.

Be certain to set aside at least five to six cents per mile for those car repairs and tire usage that will be a part of any automobile trip. For a thousand-mile trip you'll need $50 to $60; higher-mileage trips cost proportionately more.

Families with no plan often use back-to-school desires and Christmas gift giving as times to spend without counting the cost. The obvious answer to such sprees is to set aside some money each month in special Christmas and back-to-school funds. Then discipline yourself to spend only the amount you accumulated for that specific purpose.

Charles Spurgeon said, "To earn money is easy compared with spending it well." To the servants who were wise stewards of what God had entrusted to them, the Lord said, "Well done, good and faithful servant; thou hast been faithful over a few things, I will make thee ruler over many things: enter thou into the joy of thy lord" (Matthew 25:23 KJV).

Being faithful in spending what God has entrusted to you will increase your ability to give. That's a biblical principle.

Avoid waste. Whether wasting money through not keeping a budget or by paying interest on accumulated debt, the result is the same: violation of another scriptural principle.

What did Jesus command after the miracle feeding of the five thousand? ". . . Gather up the fragments that remain, that nothing be lost" (John 6:12 KJV).

Surveys reveal that approximately 10% of food purchases are thrown out in the garbage. How many meals a week do you eat of well-preserved, well-planned leftovers? What some people call "planover meals" may reduce your food spending by $15 to $30 per month.

Marjean's 2 ¢: S'mores

"*Plan*overs! Don't you mean *left*overs? Aren't you just trying to cover up last Sunday's leftovers?"

No, I truly mean *plan*overs. When I write out my menus for the week, I plan certain days to cook more of a food than I will use for one meal. For instance, I will stew a chicken and use part of it for chicken and noodles and the rest of it, say the breast, for either chicken sandwiches or chicken divan. By using a Seal-a-Meal with the plastic, boilable bags, I can store the rest of the chicken and freeze it for a meal which I have already planned for later in the week.

By doubling the meat-and-tomato sauce I make for spaghetti tonight, I can freeze the other portion for another meal of sloppy joes, chili, or a beef-and-macaroni casserole.

By planning my menus for a week and writing them on a month-at-a-glance calendar, I can arrange the foods to fit our activities, plus keep them varied. I don't want my kids to think back and say, "It must be Tuesday; we're having meatloaf."

On Wednesday morning, when I sit down with the newspaper grocery ads, my menu calendar, and my activity calendar, I think in terms of having a casserole, an old favorite, a new recipe, and fish, chicken, and beef dishes. Many mothers, in training their daughters to cook, will give one night's dinner to them to plan and prepare. I would especially encourage this during summer vacation.

After entering the main dish on each of the days of the week, taking my activities during the day and the preparation time required into consideration, I decide what vegetables and/or salad, bread, and dessert would accompany each entrée. My decisions would also be governed by the best buys listed in the ads and what I had on hand. Then, from my menus, I would think through the ingredients needed and prepare my grocery list.

Another time-saver is to picture the layout of the store and list the items in the order I come to them. This saves much backtracking. Resist, I repeat, *resist,* those impulse purchases. You haven't planned for them, and they will only raise your bill at the check stand. Remember, they are put in that special display to entice you.

Before you leave home, estimate what your bill will be. That way you won't be surprised, and you will be in control of your budget. Have an idea what you can spend each week and plan accordingly. Take a small calculator with you to keep check on yourself. This will also make you aware if the checker states a total that is completely out of line. They can make mistakes, too.

What about coupons? Clip the coupons for the items you are purchasing to your grocery list. Compare a $.10-off coupon on a popular brand item to the store brand. Many times the store brand will be cheaper than the amount of the popular brand, even after the coupon is deducted. I recently discovered a coupon organizer. I went through all the dozens of coupons I'd clipped, tossed the outdated ones and ones for items I never use, and alphabetized the others. Now I have them all together, ready to take to the store.

I keep the grocery list and menu calendar clipped to the refrigerator, so I can easily add an item when I use the last one. Then I don't forget it when I'm shopping. The menu is fun for the kids to be able to see. Many times I'd find strange writing on a future date: *tacos* or *dog-food casserole* (George's pet name for it). It meant, "Hey, Mom, I'm hungry for this." Remember to make a note of comments by the family about foods they like or don't like. I jot these down on the recipes in the books or cards.

My friend Lynn has a tradition of allowing each member of the family the privilege of selecting the menu for his or her birthday dinner. Even if it is a weird combination, the rest of the family knows it will soon be their turn, and they can choose whatever they want that night and won't get ribbed about it.

Exercise discipline. As Christians, we're told that "Bodily exercise is all right, but spiritual exercise is much more important . . ." (1 Timothy 4:8 LB). Spiritual exercise is of great importance in the spending area. Our self-control muscles need flexing several times each day.

The push-ups I need to do daily are the repetition of those four little words: *I don't need it!* My own self-control exercise program includes no desserts at noon; salad lunches two days a week; no eggs at breakfast, except one day a week; and no snacks before bed. Savings results: a bunch of calories and at least $.50 a day. Monthly savings equal $15.

Using the minimum savings of interest ($105), keeping records ($50), avoiding wasted food ($15), and self-control ($15), the reduced spending already adds up to $185 per month. Are you ready for s'more?

Buy used. S'more savings comes from buying used instead of new. You might as well get used to the word *used.* Remember that *new* only lasts one day.

Except for a house, automobiles are the biggest expenditures most families make. Note the loss of value of a car in its first seven years. Let's assume you bought the car for $7,000.

End of Year	Percentage Loss New Car	Loss of Value	Current Value
1	30%	$2,100	$4,900
2	50%	3,500	3,500
3	65%	4,550	2,450
4	75%	5,250	1,750
5	85%	5,950	1,050
6	90%	6,300	700
7	93%	6,510	490

If you buy a $7,000 new car and drive it five years, your car is worth only $1,050. Your cost of the car has been $5,950, or $1,190 annually. If you buy the same car when it is three or four years old, you can buy it for approximately $3,500. Driving it five years, you find it is worth only $490. Your cost of the car has been $3,010, or $602 annually. If you assume that added repairs will cost you $288 more than for the newer car for each of the five years, you've still saved $300 a year by buying and driving a used car. S'more savings of $25 a month. (Not counting the interest most folks pay to buy a new car.)

As a counselor for people in financial trouble, I can tell

you that most people are driving late-model cars that are a real drain on the family finances. As for me and my house, we buy them used and seem to get every place we need to go. Remember, dependability of machines is determined by proper maintenance, not by age.

So many folks fit the bumper sticker "This is the Lord's car; I bought it with my tithe."

Plan your gift giving. Gift times often lead to splurging. Someone has said we should purge the urge to splurge. How would you like to buy all the gifts you give at half-price, but have them enjoyed twice as much? My older daughter and her husband have taught me how: For her sister's birthday in August, they bought her a ski cap that they got in late March at the end-of-the-season sales. When the present was opened in August, Amy was pleased. More enjoyment resulted when she wore her cap for the first time in January.

Buy your gifts several months before you give them. This takes planning, but pays rich dividends. Multiplying all the special occasions, family birthdays, and gifts for friends, you should easily save $10 monthly. Adding to the $185 reduced spending, the used-car savings ($25), and the planned giving ($10), you have a monthly savings of $220. What would $220 monthly add to your giving to the Lord: 50%, 100%? What would $220 monthly do to your debt repayments: Double them, triple them?

Christians, let's do s'more self-control, record keeping, and doing without. Then we'll be blessed with more ability to spend whatever we have to the glory of God and more money to give to the Lord's wonderful works in this world.

Questions

Many Christians are eager to apply God's Word to their lives. As Marjean and I speak and conduct money-management seminars around the country, we're thrilled with specific questions being asked. And we've been challenged to relate the Scriptures to these questions in such a way that practical answers may be given.

Questions are grouped by subject matter. Some overlapping exists because several biblical principles may apply to one question.

ON BEING CONTENT

1. If you are content with what you have, how do you get ahead? Why work if you are content? We are told in the Bible to be content with what we *have,* not what we are (*see* Hebrews 13:5). Our task is to work heartily, as serving the Lord and not men. With a servant attitude toward our employers, we can expect to receive promotions to greater responsibilities.

2. Can a young person who feels a call to the Christian ministry be content with less than an optimum education, because of financial limitations? Paul instructs us by example to be content ". . . in every situation, whether it be a full stomach or hunger, plenty or want" (Philippians 4:12 LB). Can you imagine Paul's feeling limited because he didn't have a graduate degree from the top Christian seminary?

3. Does being content with what you have mean that we are wrong in trying to improve our present financial standing? The biblical principle is that we reap what we sow. Work is often equated with prosperity in the Bible (*see* Proverbs 14:23; 28:19). If the Lord wants to entrust you with more money, He'll most often do it through your efforts at work.

4. How do you balance being content with having a drive to do better in life and being a success at business? What is your goal? Jesus said that if you ". . . seek first his kingdom and his righteousness . . . all these things shall be yours as well" (Matthew 6:33 RSV). Obey God and obey your employer. Serve God and serve your customers. That's the formula for success.

ON BUSINESS LOANS

1. Would you explain the difference (if there is any) between personal financing and business financing and the use of debt (or borrowed) capital in each? Personal financing most often means borrowing for consumption. A family *wants* a new car, washer, furniture, or other household item. Without the cash, the item is bought; and the amount it cost is charged. Or, some budget buster crops up: repairs for the car, the furnace, water heater, or washer. With no money saved, the repair is made with borrowed money. Such borrowing is for consumption. The biblical principle of making do with your pay is being violated (*see* Luke 3:14).

Business borrowing is often for production tools. A new machine is purchased with borrowed funds. The machine will produce items which may be sold at a profit, which will be used to repay the loans. And the production machine will be security for the loan. The difference is between borrowing for consumption and borrowing for production. An illustration of business borrowing is the purchase of my computer. The use of the computer was projected to reduce our employee needs by two. These savings in labor did materialize. The wages saved could have been used to pay for the computer, had we borrowed the money to purchase it.

2. How do you start a business if you don't presently have the money? The biggest single reason people don't start businesses is that they don't have the money. Two ways to obtain the money are to borrow it or to get someone to invest in the business. Since most businesses don't make a profit until the business has been established for several months, or even years, much money is needed to pay the expenses during those first profitless months. The passages of Scripture in which debt is mentioned all appear to refer to personal debt.

3. What do you think about a farmer borrowing money ($20,000 to $50,000) for farm machinery: a tractor? One problem with borrowing is that the purchase is frequently for more than would have been bought if a certain amount of cash had been saved for the purpose. The farmer who saves $14,000 for a tractor will probably look until he finds one that he thinks will do his job for the $14,000 he has. The farmer who buys what he wants on credit may end up with the air-conditioned cab, complete with AM-FM stereo, which may not be that necessary.

On Church Finances

1. How can a local church teach its members financial responsibility? A body of believers meeting in a certain location become a local church. Financial principles for individuals are applicable to groups of God's people. The local congregation which recognizes its opportunity to give away the first part of all the church income is following the biblical principle of giving the firstfruits to the Lord. That congregation also sets an example of the giving-first principle for individual members. The congregation that pays all the bills first and then gives what is left (if any) to missions and the work of the Lord outside the local church, is setting a poor example for its members.

2. Should a church go into debt to build a new building? When I asked one of my friends, who is the stewardship leader of his denomination, what he thought about church debt, he answered, "There are two things which I dislike about church debt: There's the principal—and the interest."

Just as an individual with a need faces the question "Trust God or trust a loan?" so does a congregation.

I've seen the ministry of many churches stifled for years, while members conducted fund drive after fund drive to raise more money to pay on the mortgage of the "new building." I certainly don't subscribe to the theory I've heard advanced: A congregation that always has a debt will be the most active.

There have been many thrilling stories of God's power and provision told by congregations that trusted God for a debt-free building. And what an example such a project is to the individual members.

Christian Financial Concepts has published an excellent pamphlet titled, "Should Churches Borrow Money?" Here is a portion of that material, written by Larry Burkett.

IS CHURCH BORROWING SCRIPTURAL? This question must first be approached from the "absolutes." God's Word does not say that borrowing on the part of the "church" is forbidden.

However, borrowing represents the LEAST rather than the BEST as the church is commanded to observe. In many fellowships the existence of an indebtedness pressures them into an attitude of debt first—God second. In Proverbs 22:7, it is stated that the borrower is servant to the lender. The very act of borrowing places the church in bondage to an authority other than God's.

No where in God's Word did He ever manifest Himself through a loan. He promises to supply ALL of our needs (Philippians 4:19). Therefore the very act of borrowing is the outer sign of an inner doubt.

GOD'S BUILDING PLAN. The first time God directed a building to be constructed was in the wilderness, "Tell the sons of Israel to raise a contribution for me; from every man whose heart moves him you shall raise my contribution" (Exodus 25:2).

Thus God directed the people to give. In Exodus 36:6, Moses actually had to direct the people to stop giving. One of the unifying factors bringing the Jews into closer fellowship both with God and each other was the common goal God set before them.

In 1 Chronicles 29, David describes the collection for God's temple. It is clear that loans were not necessary to build God's house. Verse 14 describes this plan: God's people, sharing in God's plan, with God's money.

WHY NOT BORROW? The church is called by God to be unique, set apart from the world. Therefore, whatever the norm is in the world, the church must follow a totally different path.

In Philippians 2:15, we are told to hold ourselves above reproach, that we may be lights into the world of darkness. The way the church handles its money is one of the best (or poorest) testimonies. Unfortunately, many churches today operate on a nearly parallel path to secular institutions.

In a financial sense, what testimony does a church that borrows have over a secular company? Remember, the church is to be set apart, unique and established solely to God's glory.

IS BORROWING TRUSTING GOD? Does it require more faith to believe God for monthly payments or to believe He can supply according to the need "before hand"? Borrowing is a subtle way to buffer God's will for our lives. It does not necessarily represent an overt sin but it does reflect that a church is willing to accept the LEAST financially rather than the BEST. In reality the people are being denied God's blessings, both spiritually and financially. Assuming that it is God's will for a church to build, He will supply the resource to do so. When God supplies, He often provides an abundance beyond what is actually needed (2 Corinthians 9:8).

A REASONABLE COMPROMISE.   Obviously, not every church is at the same level of spiritual and financial maturity. A generation of borrowing habits are not easy to overcome and thus discerning believers must seek a reasonable compromise to avoid internal conflict.

It is clear that borrowing from unbelievers is not only a poor witness but unscriptural. In 3 John 1:7–8 believers are admonished to support those who bring the Word for "they accept nothing from the unsaved."

How can a church be a witness to God's glory and promise while they have to ask the unsaved to lend the money even for their meeting place?

A reasonable compromise is to borrow from God's people through bonds or other means. At least then God's people supply and receive His money. (The fact that this is a common means of funding building programs testifies that the resources are available.)

OUTER REFLECTION.   Remember that the way a church raises and administers its money is but an outer reflection of the inner conviction.

CHALLENGE.   It is a fact that most of the building programs that are truly needed could be funded by the Christians involved surrendering less than TEN PERCENT of their savings. They don't either because of a lack of commitment or borrowing is made too easy an alternative.

Our faith does not grow stronger unless it is tried and tested (James 1:3–4). The same is true with our financial faith.

3. Does the church have any responsibility to the welfare problem? A few years ago I heard that if every church would care for a small number of welfare recipients, no one would need to be on welfare. Since I couldn't remember the numbers, I decided to develop some figures for the county where I live. Sedgwick County, Kansas, has an average of 7,280 welfare cases a month. With 400 churches in this county, each church would need to have responsibility for 18 cases.

Think how exciting it would be if every congregation had members who considered it their responsibility to care for these few needy families in their own community. Caring would mean more than doling out the money needed to subsist. First would come individual attention, learning of needs, building a trusting relationship. Then the opportunity to share Jesus would come.

Practical needs could be met with surplus from other church members. The people on welfare could be taught to work, to plan menus, to keep a budget. We'd be taking a "cup of cold water" to the thirsty. They could be integrated into the fellowship of Jesus Christ.

What a challenge for the church of Jesus Christ. Talk about a tax revolt! With Christians meeting the needs of welfare recipients, over $150,000,000 of tax money wouldn't need to be spent, nationally.

4. How do you feel about churches and Christian organizations that ask you to give in order to pay debts accumulated when income fell? What a contrast! How different can appeals be? One Christian television personality often has emotional appeals for money to pay debts accumulated in building projects. The audience is threatened by the thought that, unless money is sent in *now,* the building project will be lost and the ministry will stop. Contrast that to a quotation from Dr. Victor B. Nelson, of the Billy

Graham Evangelistic Association. "The Billy Graham Evangelistic Association does not go into debt. We have always paid our bills on time and have expanded and proceeded only as the Lord has blessed and guided."

God's plan for His family is financial freedom. If God's people aim to be financially free, then how much more necessary it is for God's gathered family (the local church) to stay financially free.

On Giving

1. What do you mean by percentage giving? Proportionate giving means deciding on a percentage of your income to give to the Lord's work. If you adopt the tithe, you give 10% of your income. "Upon the first day of the week let every one among you lay by him in store, as God hath prospered him, that there be no gatherings when I come" (1 Corinthians 16:2 kjv). Percentage giving is a way of determining the amount you give by setting aside a percentage of your income. The size of your income is how God has prospered you.

For a number of years Marjean and I have given 15% of our income to a certain level. As God has prospered us, we have given 25% of the amount beyond that level.

We've known others who have a graduated upward scale, increasing their giving percentage with each increment in earnings.

2. Do you always have to give to the church? My answer to that question is usually another question: How do you define "the church"? My own definition of the church is much broader than the building on the corner, where we worship.

3. What is the Christian's perspective of meeting needs of the poor—the scriptural basis as individuals and as soci-

ety? Solomon said, ". . . To help the poor is to honor God" (Proverbs 14:31 LB). The Bible even says that happiness belongs to the generous man who feeds the poor (*see* Proverbs 22:9). God promises to meet our needs, if we give to the poor.

The Scriptures make it clear that Christians are directed to do more than talk about the poor (*see* James 2:15, 16). Your own local church may be involved with feeding and clothing some nearby and distant poor persons. If not, you may be led by God to give directly to the poor God puts on your doorstep or to an organization that has a ministry to the poor.

4. Would it be right to borrow money to give, say, to a church building program? Borrowing money to give presumes on God. Scripturally our giving is based on how God has prospered us, not the need of the appeal. God does not ask us to give out of what we don't have; we are to give only out of what He has entrusted to us. ". . . You will always be rich enough to be generous" (2 Corinthians 9:11 NEB). Note that Paul did not say, "Your credit will always be enough so you can give generously."

5. What do you think about faith pledges? A faith pledge is a commitment to give money that is not in sight to a certain person or organization. There are two sides to a faith pledge:

- your pledge to give.
- your faith that God will provide.

If God does not provide income beyond your expected earnings, then your pledge need not be kept.

My own faith-pledge experience has been exciting. Early last year I received, from a close Christian brother, an invitation to invest funds in an innovative new way to reach businessmen for Christ. At the time, we'd committed all the funds for the year that we could reasonably expect and had made a substantial faith pledge besides. I can remember writing to the brother and sharing that not only was I committed, but that I didn't have the faith that God would provide the pledge, let alone enough to give to his project. Oh, ye of little faith! Before the year was over, in spite of my lack of faith, God did provide the entire faith pledge, with enough left over to send a generous check to the brother, as well as some other additional gifts.

10 *Still More Unsqueezables*

I am frequently asked about investments; these questions often deal with what I think about specific investments that the person who asked the question has or that he has read or been told he should have. These investments include such things as land, bank certificates of deposit, stocks, mutual funds, foreign currencies, gold, silver, gold and silver coins, apartments, individual retirement accounts, guns, stamps, and antiques.

The answer is that I don't know about specific investments. Take land for instance. There's ghetto land, vacant lots in neighborhoods, downtown land, prime shopping-center land, suburban land, small-town land, industrial land, irrigated farmland, nonirrigated farmland, resort land, forest land, desert land, mountain land, lake land, waterfront land, swamp land, unproductive land, and all other kinds of land. Whether or not it will be a good investment depends on how much a buyer wants to pay for the land when you want to sell it. The buyers (if any are available) will depend on the potential use of the land, whether they think they can sell it for more later, and myriad other factors. Similar comments could be made about each of the more than 3,600 stocks listed on the national stock exchanges, each of the more than 780 mutual funds, each of the thousands of U.S. and foreign coins available, antiques, stamps, or most other potential investments.

The *real* question is whether or not a certain specific item is a safe place in which to invest your money and whether or not money can be made in the investment.

Let's deal with safety first. The Bible says that the only sure thing about riches is that they are *uncertain*. "Instruct those who are rich in this present world not to be conceited or to fix their hope on the uncertainty of riches, but on God, who richly supplies us with all things to enjoy" (1 Timothy 6:17 NAS).

There are no safe investments, except the treasures in heaven.

> Do not lay up for yourselves treasures upon earth, where moth and rust destroy, and where thieves break in and steal; But lay up for yourselves treasures in heaven, where neither moth nor rust destroys, and where thieves do not break in or steal; for where your treasure is, there will your heart be also.
>
> Matthew 6:19–21 NAS

At "Outlook '79," a financial seminar in New York City in January 1979, J. Anthony Boeckh, editor of *Bank Credit Analyst,* said, "There are no investments any more, in fact, only gambles."

Am I saying that the only savings the Bible tells us to have are to be put under the mattress? Not at all. But I am saying that you can only trust God for their safety and their money-making capabilities.

My Investment Priorities

Here is a list of my own priorities for the placement of my savings:

1. The business the Lord has entrusted to my management. "Develop your business first before building your house" (Proverbs 24:27 LB). A debt-free business has been our goal.

2. Our own house. Based on the same verse, our goal was to get the place where we practice Christian hospitality paid for.

3. Life insurance. I've carried life insurance since I was married, to provide for my wife and two daughters in case of my death. I was convinced of this responsibility by this statement of Paul's: "If any one does not provide for his relatives, and especially for his own family, he has disowned the faith and is worse than an unbeliever" (1 Timothy 5:8 RSV).

   Whole-life insurance premiums are a form of savings, since they are funds we are not spending. Now that our daughters are through college and on their own, we keep the life insurance, as it would allow more generous giving for Marjean in the event of my death. And it also provides for substantial gifts to the Lord's work after we both die.

4. Some readily available funds, invested in bank savings, savings and loans, and money-market mutual funds. As a small businessman, I have a responsibility to my co-workers. When the business loses money, there have to be reserves to continue to pay the expenses. ". . . for the laborer is worthy of his wages" (Luke 10:7 NAS).

5. All the income I can invest tax free. My own company has a qualified profit-sharing trust. Each eligible employee (a full-time employee with two years' service) and I have received, from company profits, 15% of our

annual salaries, tax free, into the trust, each year for the last fifteen years. Do you know of any way to earn an investment return comparable to that of not paying income taxes on the top 15% of your salary? I don't!

For this reason, I usually recommend that people take advantage of individual retirement accounts. Of course, there is then the decision of whether the money is invested in a bank, savings and loan, credit union, life-insurance company, mutual fund, or some other authorized investment medium. You'll have to seek further counsel for that specific decision.

6. Common stocks. Solomon gave us one of the Bible's soundest investment principles: "Steady plodding brings prosperity; hasty speculation brings poverty" (Proverbs 21:5 LB). For the beginning investor, a family of well-managed mutual funds may be the answer.

7. A reasonable amount of food, water, and emergency fuel is wise planning. Strikes, revolution, wars, weather crises, fuel shortages can all cause a disruption in the stocking of supermarket shelves, as well as our ability to store perishables at home. Some reasonable investment in such provisions could pay dividends in more ways than economic ones.

Savings Versus Living By Faith

Two Scriptures seem to indicate that the Bible says it is wrong to save: "For we walk by faith, not by sight" (2 Corinthians 5:7 RSV). "Lay not up for yourselves treasures upon earth . . ." (Matthew 6:19 KJV). Many people think that any financial savings shows a lack of faith in God's provision. Many also feel that any savings beyond current expenses is laying up treasures upon earth. These people conclude that all savings violates Scripture.

Scripture does teach the savings principle (*see* Proverbs 21:20; 22:3).

Admittedly there are some tensions in the Bible:

- We are to work—and to rest
- We are to save—and to live by faith
- We are to give—and to spend

The focus is to be on God, God's things, God's ways. Our aim must not be primarily on money or how we are spending it. We should want to use our lives and our resources to serve the Lord Jesus Christ. You may have noticed that the Bible has more to say about the dangers of money than about the blessings of money.

The biblical principle is for us to be savers. But we are not to store money. There's a real difference between saving and storing money. One way to test your own savings is to ask yourself whether you would refuse to meet real needs from your savings. If so, you're laying up treasures

---

Marjean's 2¢ Savings

George has already talked about the fact that a storer won't be a generous person. In a budget workshop, my friend Lynn and I were asked what a mother should do about a child who refused to spend his money, but just saved it. Lynn answered by saying she had one like that. What she had discovered, though, was that the child wouldn't spend *his* money but was willing to spend *someone else's*, that is, his parents'. I'd say he was a storer. A child needs to be taught to spend properly.

What is my part in helping in this training? First of all, I am to "fit into my husband's plans" (*see* 1 Peter 3:1). I am to support his plan of training. If I give my daughter a nickel or a dime or a dollar, then I'm saying, in effect, "Come to me if you run out of money." I'm undermining all that her father is trying to teach her.

Oh, how easy it would have been to give in. Amy

and I had spent hours, it seemed, at the shopping center, looking for a certain kind of shoes she wanted (she had her own clothing allowance). Finally we found the shoes. She tried on her size, then asked the price. Quietly she said to me, "That's too much! I don't have that much in my budget." I was tired. It was late in the day. Supper needed fixing. I wanted to say, "Oh, honey, I'll give you the difference. Just get them."

But fortunately, God revealed to me that I was to be my husband's helpmeet, a helper fit for him. I would be of no help to George or to Amy if I gave in. Consistency and example are two good teachers. Is it any wonder that both our girls have become excellent shoppers and managers of their money?

You may ask, as others have: What about the child's savings? Did you just let them build up? Yes, we let them build up and put the coins into a savings bank that registered the amount. Then we, along with the child, took the bank to the savings and loan company, where it was opened and the money deposited in our daughter's name. This is a good opportunity to teach your children about putting their money to work for them.

I would suggest that, if the child wants to purchase a big item, he be allowed to use some of his money for it. I remember Jenny, our oldest, taking her money out to buy her dog. This was the deal her father made with her when she was six years old. She could have a dog, if she saved for it. He helped her with the purchase, but that puppy was very important to her as she handed over her saved coins. But I'm afraid we didn't go far enough in teaching her that the purchase price was only the beginning.

and not really saving. The mark of a saver is generosity. The storer won't be a generous person, since there will always be a reason to store more.

Does the use of your money reflect that you live for eternity or for yourself and for now? Your check stubs will answer your own question. The Bible says, "Love not the world, neither the things that are in the world. If any man love the world, the love of the Father is not in him" (1 John 2:15 KJV).

The real key is balance: balance between giving, saving, and spending; balance between work and rest; balance between family and ministry.

Questions

ON INSURANCE

1. If we are to trust God to supply our every need, does it show a lack of trust to put money into such things as life and health insurance, instead of putting that money into Christian charities and programs? The Bible does say that God will supply our needs. There's no reason that supply can't come through various kinds of insurance, however.

Solomon said, "A prudent man foresees the difficulties ahead and prepares for them; the simpleton goes blindly on and suffers the consequences" (Proverbs 22:3 LB).

God's Word never tells us we won't be sick or suffer from disease. Medical insurance provides a plan for the prudent man to pay for illness. By making a monthly premium payment, a person is budgeting for future medical expenses. I carry medical insurance and also provide part of the premium for my co-workers to obtain good major-medical coverage at the lowest group rates.

Life insurance is a way to make provision for your family in case of the death of the wage earner. The person who cares enough for his family to purchase life insurance is expressing a unique brand of love.

One woman who came to me for financial counseling told me this story. At the time her daughter was preparing to leave for college, her husband died. His life insurance made it possible for the woman to buy a house in the college town, where she and her daughter could live together. Since the woman had eye trouble and couldn't work, the life insurance made the difference between a poverty existence and continuing a life-style similar to their past one. I've never seen anyone who was collecting life-insurance proceeds who could be anything but thankful for the unselfishness of the deceased loved one.

Disability insurance can be equally important. A far better name for it is income-protection insurance. When the wage earner becomes unable to work, due to sickness or accident, after a waiting period of several days to several months, the insurance begins to provide income payments.

My own company carries such insurance for our company family. Scripturally I have a responsibility to them to meet their needs in times of crisis. What a blessing to know that the incomes of several disabled employees have continued long after they were unable to work.

ON SPENDING

1. How do you advise people to handle medical expenses that go over their ability to pay? Talk over your situation with your medical creditors. Work out a plan for the steady payment of those medical bills, using some of each month's earnings.

A newspaper-route man used to come to our collection agency every Monday before 8:00 A.M. and leave ten dimes on the counter. Believe it or not, he paid off a hospital bill of several hundred dollars with those regular dimes.

2. *How do you overcome impulsive buying?* Cut up all credit cards. Close all charge accounts. When you go out shopping, carry only enough cash to buy what you have gone after. Leave your checkbook at home. Have a prayer partner with whom you share your opportunity for the Lord to strengthen you. Be accountable to your prayer partner for all money spent.

3. *What if both partners in a marriage don't agree about spending money?* The Bible says that they can't walk together unless they agree (*see* Amos 3:3). There will be arguments, tension, and often open warfare. The usual result is a pile of debts that they can't agree how to pay. Such pressures will often result in divorce.

I often tell people thinking about divorce, "If you think you have money problems now, just wait until you get your divorce. Then you'll know what *real* financial problems are. The chances are that you'll both live in poverty the rest of your lives."

My straight talk seldom stops the divorce, however, because these people have already made up their minds, and the facts will not affect them.

ON TAXES

1. *How do you know how much to allow for the federal income tax and the state income tax?* You can estimate your taxes based on your estimated income. Every employer should have a current year's withholding table for withholding federal and state taxes from incomes, based on various pay periods, amount of earnings, and number of dependents. Multiply the deductions for each tax by the number of paydays in the year, and you should have a fairly accurate estimate of your year's taxes.

I'm amazed, every year, at the number of people who discover in April that they owe substantial amounts of income taxes from the previous year. Be sure to check each year to see how your income tax withholding or estimates are measuring against your tax liability. Advance planning in this area can help you avoid severe unexpected financial needs.

On Wills

1. Is a lawyer necessary to draw up a will? Do you need a surgeon to do surgery? I can't imagine a do-it-myself will or my will being copied from a friend's will (which may have been drawn up by a lawyer). Would I take my friend's prescribed pills?

A good book on financial planning has been written by a Christian attorney and his wife. It's called *Successful Financial Planning,* by George and Margaret Hardisty (Fleming H. Revell Company, Old Tappan, New Jersey, 1978).

2. In writing a will, do you think that the lawyer should be a Christian? The preference is to deal with a Christian, because the Psalmist indicates that we'll be blessed if we walk not in the counsel of the ungodly (*see* Psalms 1:1). But if there are no Christians around, pick a competent attorney. Not all attorneys are competent estate planners. Inquire of your accountant, insurance officer, or bank trust officer for the name of an attorney who has specialized in estate planning.

3. What should be included in a will? Read George Hardisty's book and/or ask your attorney. It is *your* will. Let it reflect *you.* Since wills are read by several people, and often read for generations, in abstracts, some Christians even include their personal testimonies.

On Work

1. Do you think a person with family responsibilities should quit a job because he believes God is calling him to study for

the ministry? The first question I would ask is, "What kind of ministry does the person with family responsibilities have where he is?"

- Is his marriage alive and well?
- Is he the priest in his own family?
- Are his children being taught by conduct and example in prayer and study of God's Word?
- Is he functioning as a multiplying, fruitful Christian where he is now working?
- Are people being led to Christ?
- Are Christians being encouraged and shown how to grow?
- Are the fruits of the Spirit so evident in the person's life that co-workers are coming to him for counsel?

I've heard Dr. Richard Halverson say many times, "If you aren't functioning for Jesus Christ where you are, you probably won't function for Christ where you're not."

If your work life is fruitful now and you sense God's leading to study for the ministry, seek godly counsel. Also seek the counsel of your own family. And be certain that your wife's honest feelings are being communicated to you.

OH, THOSE COLLEGE LOANS

1. What about students whose basic expenses come to more money than they can earn in part-time work? Students, too, face situations in which expenses exceed income. Several alternatives exist for you:

    a. If you are trusting God for the money to get you through school, and there just isn't enough money, you could conclude that, at this time, the Lord wants you someplace other than school.

    b. You could quit trusting God and trust a loan to "tide you over."

c. You could pray for God to multiply your willingness to work. With studying and part-time work occupying the bulk of your time, you see no way to add to your work. Here's where ". . . my God will supply every need of yours . . ." (Philippians 4:19 rsv) comes in.

Tell the Lord you're willing to be in school or out, as He leads (*see* Psalms 32:8). Ask the Lord for income that will be sufficient to pay for your schooling (*see* Matthew 7:7). Be alert to opportunities for you to earn while you learn. Many jobs today require your presence more than your work. House-sitting while people are away earns you income while you have time to study. Funeral homes usually require someone on duty at night, to answer the telephone.

Make use of your school breaks. Thanksgiving, Christmas, and spring break offer times for extra earnings. By staying at school and working, instead of traveling home or going skiing, you increase income and decrease expenses.

2. *What do you think about school loans?* My collection agency has tried to collect over 20,000 delinquent school loans that have been turned over to us by almost 100 colleges.

Most of these loans were granted in the haste of college registration. Seldom is much counseling done about the responsibility of repayment. My experience is that most students don't really understand what they are facing, when they sign a note to pay back a large debt, plus interest, over a ten-year period after they graduate.

The world cries loudly, "One easy payment!" Have you ever seen an "easy payment"? I haven't. All payments are hard—a burden on the budget. Such loans often cause problems in marriage relationships, to say nothing of the financial strain.

On a delinquent account, in our office, our first telephone contact produced a violent reaction from a girl who owed money to a Christian college. She raved about how she had already paid $200 and that her semester at school certainly hadn't been worth even that amount. She was hostile to us and critical of the college. She even said that school officials had lied to her about the cost of the school. Her tirade ended by her claiming that she would not pay the $1,200 the school said she owed and that the school wouldn't sue her, since it would not be a Christian act for the school to file suit against her, a Christian.

A review of her file at school showed a radical change in her attitude since she had married. Before that time she had made regular, small payments on the loan. With each payment she had written to thank the school for her education. She had also acknowledged her financial obligation to the school and promised faithful payments for as long as it took to pay off what she owed.

Then came the dramatic change. This is just one example of what the trauma and pressure can do to young couples with school debts. As they turn their thoughts toward things for their home, they easily forget their promises of the past. How easy it is, in the process, to turn away from the Lord, as well. "For the love of money is the first step toward all kinds of sin. Some people have even turned away from God because of their love for it, and as a result have pierced themselves with many sorrows" (1 Timothy 6:10 LB).

3. What do you do when people make unusual requests for your money: college students who have run out of money and want to borrow some? Students share with nonstudents those occasions when others approach us for temporary loans to meet some emergency.

God may choose to use you to meet a brother's or sister's

need. If, after prayer, you have peace about *giving* the person the money, then give it joyfully.

My own experience is that God often uses finances to teach people spiritual lessons. Unfaithfulness with finances often results in a person's being in a position of real need. By looking to the *Lord* to meet that need, they learn valuable lessons of prayer and faith. By looking to other *people* to meet the need, they miss such lessons and spiritual growth.

Some students will turn to other students, instead of admitting to their parents that they are broke. You may have heard about this letter exchange between a father and his college-student son: "Dear Dad: No mon, no fun, your son." "Dear Son: So sad, too bad, your dad."

I've had to ask the Lord's forgiveness, more than once, for giving someone money and preventing the work God was doing in his life. When the repossessor came to my office to pick up an employee's car, I interfered. Money the Lord had entrusted to me was used to prevent the repossession. I felt that I was helping my employee. Later I discovered that she could not afford her car, but was unwilling to give it up. But, God, in spite of me and of her, allowed the car to be totaled some days later. And that was an even tougher way to give it up!

By Students

1. What if your parents really want you to take out a loan for college, and you have explained to them you don't want to and have shown them why (biblical reasons) and prayed, but they still feel you should take out the loan to finish school? Take out the loan. God will bless your obedience to your parents. The Bible commands you to obey your parents and ends with the promise "that it may be well with you" (Ephesians 6:1–3 NEB).

2. If you commit yourself to supporting certain ministries, and your income changes, what should you do? Lower your support. We are to be proportionate givers: income up—giving up; income down—giving down.

3. What kind of records should I keep, as a college student? Keep a budget. Learning to plan your spending will probably mean more to you than most of your college courses. A sample budget for the school year, along with projected income sources, might look like this for a state school:

1979 SAMPLE STUDENT BUDGET

	Student Pays All (except car maint.)	Parents Pay Tuition & Books	Fill in Your Amt.
Giving	36.00	26.00	
Shelter	100.00	100.00	
Food	50.00	50.00	
Clothing	20.00	20.00	
Education (tuition + books + fees)	84.00	——	
Spiritual Growth	25.00	25.00	
Gifts	5.00	5.00	
Transportation (Parents' car—gas only)	24.00	24.00	
Personal Allowances	15.00	15.00	
Other	0.00	0.00	
Per Month Total	359.00	265.00	
Per Year Total	4,308.00	3,180.00	

Estimated Income:
Summer Earnings   +
Scholarship/Grant   +
Part-time School Job +
Parents   +
Other   +
                Total
Minus per year Total _____

  Estimated
    Surplus (+)
    Deficit (−)

4. What should we give if we have no income? Tithe your time.

5. If a young Christian couple is planning on marriage, would it be advisable for them to remain financially independent of each other, or should the girl begin to submit her financial freedom to her fiancé by asking his advice before spending, or should she continue to spend without consulting him? Finances are an important part of marriage. You can learn a lot about each other by delving into money matters together, before you marry.

ON TRAINING CHILDREN

1. How do you handle budgets for teenagers? The goal of a child's budget is to help him learn to be a responsible money manager. Our daughters started out with the budget-box planned spending. The three-box cash system worked for several years. Every allowance was divided among the three boxes (*church, save,* and *spend*) according to our agreed-on plan.

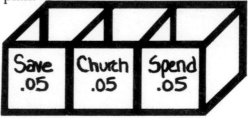

Have a kid-proof bank to put each week's savings in when the next week's allowances are given. Plan times during the year to open the bank and take the child to a savings institution with you, to deposit his savings in his account. You can also use the account as a depository for birthday cash from relatives and other unexpected sources of funds.

Let his spending money be sufficient for reasonable childish desires. But be sure that he doesn't have a ready source of cash from you when he is out of money.

For our family, the first graduation from the budget boxes took place with a clothing budget. During their early teens, we helped our daughters open a checking account with their own checks. Each month we gave them a check to deposit in that clothing account. They understood that there would be no other clothing funds, unless they earned the money themselves.

By the time the children are in high school, they should be ready for a more involved but realistic budget. A full teenage spending plan could include church, savings, clothes, gifts, health, education, fun, and transportation. Each category could include some or all of these items:

- *Church:* giving at church, Sunday school, youth groups, school drives, United Way, a needy friend or relative.
- *Savings:* money saved for college, a future purchase, or an investment.
- *Clothes:* clothing, jewelry, cleaning, repairs, shoes.
- *Gifts:* all gifts for Christmas, birthdays, showers, special days such as Valentine's, Mother's Day, and any others.
- *Health:* personal drug items such as toothpaste, shampoo, and tissues. Ordinarily the parents pay for medical treatment and prescription drugs.
- *Education:* school plays, supplies during the year (not books), library fines.
- *Food:* school lunches, pizza after games.
- *Fun:* movies, athletic events, between-meal snacks, retreats.
- *Transportation:* if driving the family car, sharing the cost of the gas; bus fare; bicycle repairs.

A budget in college could be similar to that of the high schooler, with some items added. They'll need stamps, stationery, laundry money, and myriad other items, if they live away from home.

2. What did your daughters do with money they earned while they were on a budget? Our daughters divided the earnings according to a predetermined plan. A good division is among giving, saving, and spending. An excellent plan is to give 10%, save 40%, and spend 50%. What they spend *their* money on with that kind of plan should be up to *them*.

11 *Victory Over the Squeeze*

One evening, while I was working on the last pages of this book, the phone rang. My friend John excitedly blurted out that his income-tax refund had just arrived and that the check totaled $500 more than his tax return had listed.

"Best of all," John said, "The amount is just enough to make the last payment on all my debts. I'll be *financially free!*"

John deserved to shout. Four years earlier, as a brand-new Christian, he sat on my couch. He owed $17,000 and owned some clothes, golf clubs, and a T.V. set. He was pumping gas long hours each week, while interest on the debt kept it growing like spring dandelions.

You Can Have the Victory

During the past few years, many have called and written to share the thrill and rejoicing they experienced as they became financially free.

Some quotes of theirs may encourage you in your struggle to become UNSQUEEZED.

From a college professor: "When you were here, we owed $1,400 on Master Charge and Visa—and it was getting higher. In our seven years of married life, it was the first time we had 'lost control' of any area of our finances. We needed your *warning.* And we heeded your advice. We had 'plastic surgery.' As of today we owe Master Charge and Visa *nothing!* We are rejoicing.

"Also we moved our giving above the 10% mark for the first time. True, it's only gone to 13%; but I'm really excited about the small gain."

From a young pastor: "God has used you to motivate us to commit our lives and finances to Him in a fuller and more complete way. Every time I fail to follow the principles I learned from you, God convicts me and brings me back into obedience."

From a man newly married for the second time: "I am writing to thank you for your book *You Can Be Financially Free,* which I purchased from a Christian bookstore, and to let you know how much it has helped our family. For my wife and me, this makes our second marriage. In each case in our first marriages, there was overspending, no budgeting and little planning of any kind.

"Consequently, when my new wife and I met, each of us was heavily in debt. When we were married last April, combined, we owed around $6,000 on eleven different accounts. This did not include the payment on our mobile home, since I have considered that in the same terms as buying a regular house. We have established a goal of completely getting out of debt, with the exception of the mobile home. At this time, we have reduced this debt to $3,200 and now only owe on five accounts. We followed many of your guidelines and suggestions in your book. By the end of 1979 we plan to have our goal reached of being debt-free. We have also been able to save regularly, although we have had some occasions to withdraw. But we have learned the importance of a systematic savings plan. Also we tithe our incomes, along with giving to other causes in addition to our tithing."

From a young married man with three children: "When I first started your class, I quickly became aware just how deeply in debt I was. It was a shock! After making a budget outline, I found out that I wasn't making enough to pay the bills each month. Gradually I was going deeper in debt.

After having a private session with you, I received ideas that would help me on my way to becoming financially free: ideas like cutting back from three telephones to one; cutting back from two cars to one; also, keeping a budget! But the best idea that I received from the class was to do it through the Lord Jesus Christ. And I'm glad to report it sure has helped.

"You told us to set a goal for the amount of time we needed to get out of debt. My goal was one year. I was in debt $7,000, to start. As of today I'm still $2,000 in debt. To a certain extent I have succeeded in cutting it back quite a bit, but I also failed, because I know if I had disciplined myself better and kept my budget going at all times, I would have succeeded completely. I learned a good lesson.

"But I'm not discouraged. I know that, being patient and dedicated, I will be financially free of debt. Thank you both, George and Marjean, for your help and your financial class. And best of all, thank the *Lord Jesus Christ!*"

What these people had in common was putting into practice in their lives instructions from God's Word: "But be doers of the word, and not hearers only, deceiving yourselves" (James 1:22 RSV). They had become doers of the Word.

In each case, they decided to obey God's Word by:

- purposing to live within their incomes and avoiding new debts.
- setting up and following a financial budget.
- facing the facts about cars and houses.
- trusting God by giving Him the first 10% of all their incomes.

Everyone we have counseled who has chosen to obey these principles in Scripture has experienced a special blessing in facing the financial SQUEEZE. That blessing, of course, comes as no surprise to me, since God promises to bless those who act on His Word: "But he who looks into the perfect law, the law of liberty, and perseveres, being no hearer that forgets but a doer that acts, he shall be blessed in his doing" (James 1:25 RSV). How about you? Are you afraid of the SQUEEZE? Are you caught in the SQUEEZE? Ask God to bring to your mind what you know He says about money management—about saving, spending, debt, giving, keeping records, and getting the facts.

Now, begin, a step at a time, to obey His principles. You'll experience God's personal blessing in your life, and you'll begin to be a shining light for Jesus Christ, as you have victory over the financial SQUEEZE, to His glory.

Additional Reading

Bonner, Mickey. *The Scriptural Way to Get Out of Debt.* Mickey Bonner, 1977.

Bowman, George M. *How to Succeed With Your Money.* Chicago: Moody Press, 1974.

Bowman, George M. *Clockwise: Make Every Minute Count.* Old Tappan, NJ: Fleming H. Revell Co., 1979.

Burkett, Larry. *Your Finances in Changing Times.* San Bernardino, CA: Campus Crusade for Christ, 1975.

Burkett, Larry. *Family Financial Planning Workbook.* Norcross, GA: Christian Financial Concepts, 1977.

Burkett, Larry. *God's Principles of Handling Money.* Norcross, GA: Christian Financial Concepts, 1975.

Burkett, Larry. *What Husbands Wish Their Wives Knew About Money.* Wheaton, IL: Victor Books, 1977.

Cantelon, Willard. *The Day the Dollar Dies: Biblical Prophecy of a New World System in the End Times.* Plainfield, NJ: Logos International, 1973.

Cantelon, Willard. *Money Master of the World.* Plainfield, NJ: Logos International, 1976.

Clason, George S. *The Richest Man in Babylon.* New York: Hawthorne Books, 1955.

Copeland, Kenneth. *The Laws of Prosperity.* Greensburg, PA: Manna Christian Outreach, 1974.

Dayton, Howard L. *Your Money: Frustration or Freedom?* Wheaton, IL: Tyndale House Publisher, Inc., 1979.

Dunn, David. *Try Giving Yourself Away.* Englewood Cliffs, NJ: Prentice-Hall, Inc., 1970.

Eggerichs, Fred, with Palmer, Bernard W. *A Bag Without Holes.* Minneapolis, MN: Bethany Fellowship, Inc., 1975.

Enlow, David, and Enlow, Dorothy. *Saved From Bankruptcy.* Chicago: Moody Press, 1975.

Fooshee, George, Jr., *You Can Be Financially Free.* Old Tappan, NJ: Fleming H. Revell Company, 1976.

Ford, George L. *All the Money You Need: A Guidebook for Christian Financial Planning.* Waco, TX: Word, Inc., 1976.

Galloway, Dale E. *There Is a Solution to Your Money Problems.* Glendale, CA: Regal Books, 1977.

Hancock, Maxine. *Living on Less and Liking It More.* Chicago: Moody Press, 1977.

Hardisty, George, and Hardisty, Margaret. *Successful Financial Planning.* Old Tappan, NJ: Fleming H. Revell Company, 1978.

Kauffman, Milo. *Stewards of God.* Scottdale, PA: Herald Press, 1975.

King, Bill, and King, Pat. *Money Talks: It Says Good-by.* Lynnwood, WA: Women's Aglow Fellowship, 1977.

MacGregor, Malcolm, with Baldwin, Stanley G. *Your Money Matters.* Minneapolis, MN: Bethany Fellowship, Inc., 1977.

MacGregor, Malcolm, with Baldwin, Stanley G. *Financial Planning Guide for Your Money Matters.* Minneapolis. MN: Bethany Fellowship, Inc., 1978.

Olford, Stephen. *The Grace of Giving.* Grand Rapids, MI: Zondervan Publishing House, 1972.

Peppin, Paul G., with Roddy, Lee. *The Family Necessary Book.* Old Tappan, NJ: Fleming H. Revell Company, 1977.

Taylor, Jack R. *God's Miraculous Plan of Economy.* Nashville, TN: Broadman Press, 1975.

Temple, George. *Is Anyone in Charge?* El Reno, OK: Temple Press, 1979.

Werning, Waldo J. *Where Does the Money Go?* Winona Lake, IN: Light & Life Press, 1972.

Whitt, Peggy. *The Good Idea How to Save Money Book.* Blue Ridge Summit, PA: TAB Books, 1978.

Yohn, Rick. *God's Answers to Financial Problems.* Irvine, CA: Harvest House Publishers, 1978.

Young, Amy Ross. *It Only Hurts Between Paydays.* Denver, CO: Accent Books, 1975.

Young, Samuel. *Giving and Living.* Grand Rapids, MI: Baker Book House, 1976.

Scripture Index

Readers of *You Can Be Financially Free* have frequently told us how they used the scriptural references about money and possessions. An enlarged index is included, to aid you in your personal search of the Scriptures dealing with financial topics.

Counsel Psalms 1:1; Psalms 16:7; Psalms 32:8; Proverbs 2:9; Proverbs 8:33; Proverbs 10:21; Proverbs 13:17; Proverbs 15:22; Jeremiah 33:3

Debt Leviticus 26:13; 2 Kings 4:1; Psalms 37:21; Proverbs 1:17, 18; Proverbs 3:27, 28; Proverbs 22:7; Matthew 6:12; Luke 3:14; Romans 13:8

Discipline Matthew 7:13, 14; Luke 9:51; 2 Corinthians 8:11; 1 Timothy 4:8; Hebrews 12:11

Encouragement Psalms 42:11; Proverbs 25:13

Faithfulness Matthew 25:23; Luke 16:10, 11

Freedom John 8:32

Get the Facts 2 Kings 4:2; Proverbs 1:29, 31; Proverbs 14:8; Proverbs 14:15; Proverbs 18:13; Proverbs 19:2; Proverbs 23:23; Proverbs 27:23, 24; Mark 6:37, 38; Luke 14:31, 32; James 1:5

Gospel Mark 1:15; John 3:16; Revelation 3:20

Guidance Psalms 25:4, 5; Psalms 32:8; Psalms 143:8; Isaiah 30:21; Jeremiah 8:4, 5; Mark 1:35

Helpmeet Proverbs 14:1; Proverbs 31:10–31; Amos 3:3; 1 Corinthians 11:3; Ephesians 5:22, 24; 1 Peter 3:1

Hope Romans 8:28; Romans 15:4

Inheritance Proverbs 13:22; Ecclesiastes 2:18, 19; Luke 15:11–31

Interest Exodus 22:25; Leviticus 25:36; Deuteronomy 23:19; Psalms 15:5

Investments Matthew 6:19–21 Matthew 24:35; Matthew 25:14–30; Mark 4:19; 2 Timothy 2:4; 2 Peter 3:10

Source of Wealth   Deuteronomy 8:18; 1 Chronicles 29:12; 2 Chronicles 16:9; Psalms 24:1; Psalms 34:9; Psalms 50:12, 14, 15; Proverbs 8:20, 21; Malachi 3:10–12; Matthew 6:33; Matthew 7:7; Matthew 21:22; Luke 18:27; John 10:10; John 16:24; 2 Corinthians 9:8; Ephesians 3:20; Philippians 4:6, 7; Philippians 4:19; 1 Timothy 6:17

Speculations   (*see* Investments) Proverbs   21:5; Ecclesiastes 5:15–17

Strength   Psalms 46:10; Philippians 4:13

Success   Psalms 1:2, 3

Unity   Ecclesiastes 4:9; Amos 3:3; Romans 12:16

Victory   Proverbs 13:19

Vision   Proverbs 29:18; Luke 18:27; Galatians 6:7; Galatians 6:9; Revelation 22:11

Waiting   Psalms 27:14; Psalms 40:1–3; Isaiah 40:31; Isaiah 52:12; John 11:6

Waste   Luke 15:13; John 6:12

Work   Genesis 1:1; Genesis 2:2, 3; Exodus 23:12; 1 Chronicles 28:20; 2 Chronicles 31:21; Nehemiah 4:6; Proverbs 12:9; Proverbs 12:24; Proverbs 13:11; Proverbs 13:19; Proverbs 14:23; Proverbs 28:19; Ecclesiastes 5:12; Luke 10:7; 1 Corinthians 10:31; 1 Corinthians 14:40; Philippians 2:13; Colossians 3:23; 2 Timothy 2:15; 2 Peter 1:10

Worldliness   Deuteronomy 8:11; Proverbs 11:28; Proverbs 30:8, 9; Ecclesiastes 5:12; Mark 4:19; 1 John 2:15, 16